LOOK AGAIN PICTURES

for Language Development and Lifeskills

Pictures and text designed and developed by

Judy Winn-Bell Olsen

City College of San Francisco

Illustrated by

Timothy White

Development editors: Helen Munch, Joan Wolfgang

Production editors: Carol Ann Brimeyer, Naomi Steinfeld

Designer and production manager: E. Carol Gee

Production coordinator: Elizabeth Tong

©1998 Alta Book Center Publishers

14 Adrian Court

Burlingame, California 94010 USA

Phone: 800 ALTA/ESL • 650.692.1285 (Int'l)

Fax: 800 ALTA/FAX • 650.692.4654

Email ALTAESL@AOL.COM • Website: WWW.ALTAESL.COM

Printed in the United States of America

ISBN 1-882483-70-7

Original Copyright 1984 by Alemany Press

Dedication

to my parents: Jean and Don Bell
and
Howard and Stella Winn

Acknowledgements

Many people in the San Francisco Bay Area helped with this project along the way. Chris Bunn first gave me the idea, many years ago. Marge Ryder and Yvonne Safwat kept me at it this past year. Janet Thornburg and Carol Gee were extremely helpful in finalizing the format. Polishing of the pictures and some ideas for exercises came from field testing and comments by Karen Bachelor de Garcia, Pat Brenneke, Bruce Coleman, Linda Cornejo, Terry Doyle, Jo Egenes, Carole Glanzer, Joan Hanford Young, Alice Hines, Judy Kaplan, Betty Kissilove, Shirley LaMere, Susan Lawson, Kim Lee, Clare Morgano, Melanie O'Hare, John Oliver, Roger Olsen, Betsy Portaro, Linda Schurer, Sherry Thomas, Jack Wigfield, and Betty Wilkinson. Thanks to K. Lynn Savage for her comments on lifeskills, and to Peggy Doherty for her help in implementing the field testing.

As the manuscript neared completion, editors Helen Munch and Joan Wolfgang were immensely supportive and helpful. And throughout the design and implementation of this project, husband Roger E. W-B Olsen's vast reserves of patience were tapped repeatedly, but never ran dry.

I cannot say enough for the talent and flexibility of artist Timothy White, who took my ideas for scenes and characters and gave them life. An exciting part of this project for me was watching my crude sketches and verbal descriptions take on shape and detail as Timothy wielded his pencils and pens. I am particularly grateful for his continued patient willingness to redraw and redesign pictures according to my requests ("Just one more time, only this time could you change this, and put that over there, and move these two closer together, and...and...?") Much of the magic that is in LOOK AGAIN PICTURES developed as Tim drew again...and again...and again.

Table of Contents

Introduction
- *LOOK AGAIN PICTURES:* What It Is and Who It's For 1
- How to Use *LOOK AGAIN PICTURES* Most Effectively 1
  - Finding the Differences 1
    - Procedure 2
    - Very Beginning Classes 2
    - High Beginning-Low Intermediate Classes 2
    - Intermediate Classes 2
    - Advanced Classes 2
  - Discussing the Context 3
  - Language Functions 4
  - Lifeskills Extensions 5
  - Further Language Development 5

Picture 1: A Coffee Shop 6
- *Differences*
- *Context Questions*
- *Language Functions*:
  - taking an order; ordering; expressing
  - displeased surprise; expressing surprise/apologizing
- *Lifeskills Extensions*:
  - ordering from a menu; checking the
  - bill/figuring the tip
- *Further Language Development*:
  - What <u>would</u> you like? vs. What <u>do</u> you like?;
  - scrambled sentences exercise

Picture 2: A Coffee Shop Kitchen 10
- *Differences*
- *Context Questions*
- *Language Functions*:
  - exclaiming and warning; responding to
  - a warning; asking for specific job information;
  - giving specific job information; asking about job
  - experience; giving job experience
- *Lifeskills Extensions*:
  - matching exercises and story problems for
  - "Help Wanted" ads; job application forms; workers'
  - rights posters
- *Further Language Development*:
  - cloze exercises

Picture 3: A Clothing Sale **14**
    Differences
    Context Questions
    Language Functions:
        asking for clarification; expressing doubt;
        hedging or polite put-offs; expressing disapproval;
        reassuring; expressing amusement/teasing;
        expressing approval
    Lifeskills Extensions:
        reading ads (determining percent
        discounts); comparing ads; contact assignment to
        check prices; story problems for reading,
        computation, and discussion; discussing sales,
        discount stores, and sales tax
    Further Language Development:
        dialog activities; reported speech;
        speaker identification; cloze/scrambled sentence
        exercises; reading, grammar, and controlled
        composition exercise; pronunciation practice:
        final -s/-es

Picture 4: Exchanges and Layaways **18**
    Differences
    Context Questions
    Language Functions:
        eliciting customer response; making customer
        complaints by describing defects and malfunctions;
        describing options; asking for clarification
        of layaway terms
    Lifeskills Extensions:
        discussing exchanges and returns policies;
        comparing purchasing methods
    Further Language Development:
        too vs. enough exercises; passive voice
        exercise; pronunciation practice: final -ed

Picture 5: Getting on the Bus **22**
    Differences
    Context Questions
    Language Functions:
        asking directions; giving directions;
        asking for change or the time; responding politely
        to an easy request; complaining; making small talk
    Lifeskills Extensions:
        comparing transportation systems; story problems
        using maps and schedules; listening
        comprehension/dialogs: transportation
        information services

Further Language Development:
    pattern drills; understanding pronouns and making
    <u>Yes/No</u> questions; simple present tense and
    frequency adverbs; scrambled sentences with simple
    present tense and frequency adverbs

Picture 6: Riding on the Bus **26**
    Differences
    Context Questions:
        teacher-guided student questioning exercise
    Language Functions:
        expressing displeased surprise; apologizing; asking
        for clarification; giving clarification; offering
    Lifeskills Extensions:
        discussing tokens, transfers, passes; story
        problems using math
    Further Language Development:
        adjective placement before nouns; <u>-ed</u> vs.
        <u>-ing</u> adjectives; modal auxiliaries

Picture 7: A Supermarket Aisle **30**
    Differences
    Context Questions
    Language Functions:
        politely asking strangers for reasonable action;
        asking a friend for an opinion or preference;
        expressing mild disagreement or disapproval;
        expressing strong disagreement or disapproval;
        reprimanding children
    Lifeskills Extensions:
        price checking exercise; comparison shopping
        exercises
    Further Language Development:
        listening comprehension using picture grids

Picture 8: A Supermarket Checkout Counter **34**
    Differences
    Context Questions
    Language Functions:
        politely requesting an easy favor; complying
        with an easy request; expressing dismay;
        expressing annoyance indirectly; expressing
        helpful concern
    Lifeskills Extensions:
        categorizing meat and poultry; reading for
        information and filling out a check-cashing card;
        categorizing cleaning products by their use
    Further Language Development:
        quantifiers; dialog development through paraphrase

Picture 9: A Clinic Waiting Room 38

    Differences

    Context Questions

    Language Functions:

        answering a business call/giving information;

        asking for health information on the telephone;

        reassuring and encouraging; asking for clarification

        of procedure; requesting more specific information

    Lifeskills Extensions:

        listing local clinics and emergency hospitals

        (using information questions and map practice);

        roleplaying emergency calls

    Further Language Development:

        vocabulary-picture matching exercises

Picture 10: Talking to the Doctor 42

    Differences

    Context Questions

    Language Functions:

        asking for information about someone's illness;

        describing symptoms of an illness; giving instructions;

        asking for clarification; complaining; comforting

    Lifeskills Extensions:

        understanding labels on prescription and

        non-prescription medication

    Further Language Development:

        vocabulary activity; four-by-four dialogs exercise

Picture 11: Outside an Apartment 46

    Differences

    Context Questions

    Language Functions:

        expressing doubt; expressing hope; asking for

        information; giving information

    Lifeskills Extensions:

        understanding rental ads (discussing

        abbreviations); story problems using rental ads

    Further Language Development:

        vocabulary and dialog exercises (using Yes/No

        and Either/Or questions); What/How-questions

Picture 12: Inside an Apartment 50

    Differences

    Context Questions

    Language Functions:

        asking for information; giving information; hedging;

        indirectly requesting changes; reassuring

    Lifeskills Extensions/Further Language Development:

        TPR faucet-repair sequences; a letter of complaint

Picture 13: A Bank Line **54**

Differences

Context Questions

Language Functions:

requesting routine service in a business
transaction; responding to a request for
routine service; complaining; making small
talk with an acquaintance

Lifeskills Extensions:

examining bank forms (checks, deposit slips,
and withdrawal slips); comparing banks and
S&L institutions

Further Language Development:

listening comprehension and vocabulary exercise;
contrast of "wish" and "hope"

Picture 14: A Bank Desk **58**

Differences

Context Questions

Language Functions:

congratulating; expressing pleasure; expressing
dismay; calling attention to a particular place;
indicating urgent need; requesting routine service
in a business transaction; responding to a request
for routine service

Lifeskills Extensions:

filling out bank forms (account and loan
applications); reading bank/S&L brochures

Further Language Development:

inferential reading-skill exercise
(character-dialog matching)

Picture 15: At an Airport **62**

Differences

Context Questions

Language Functions:

greetings; asking for service information;
giving service information; asking information
of a stranger; giving information to a stranger

Lifeskills Extensions:

comparing methods of transportation; story
problems to determine transportation method;
letter-writing exercise (travel information)

Further Language Development:

listening comprehension (true/false);
vocabulary/alphabet list contest; regular
and irregular verbs; future or past tenses;
present perfect and past tenses; "if" and
unreal conditional

Picture 16: Inside a Terminal **66**

Differences

Context Questions

Language Functions:

bidding for attention from a parent; requesting
reasonable action from a customer in a service
encounter; complying with a reasonable request;
making small talk while waiting for something

Lifeskills Extensions:

reading schedules; discussing baggage allowances for
different kinds of travel; comparing travel fares and costs

Further Language Development:

student-monitored dictations; intonation practice:
Yes/No, WH–, and "Or" questions; listening
comprehension exercises

Picture 17: Motor Vehicle Registration **70**

Differences

Context Questions

Language Functions:

giving instructions; giving positive feedback;
responding to positive feedback; completing
a business transaction; making small talk
(trying to impress a member of the opposite sex)

Lifeskills Extensions:

using driver's manuals; interviewing students
with new licenses

Further Language Development:

vocabulary of increase/decrease; common connectives
exercise; nouns used as modifiers

Picture 18: A Driving Test **74**

Differences

Context Questions

Language Functions:

expressing anxiety; reassuring; expressing
curiosity; giving negative information with
mitigation; expressing disappointment; asking for
clarification; encouraging; expressing impatience

Lifeskills Extensions:

discussing consumer-related topics (cars: kinds,
parts, new vs. used, car-related problems)

Further Language Development:

listening comprehension exercise; review
of relative clause types

Picture 19: A Furniture Store **78**

Differences
Context Questions
Language Functions:
offering an opinion; attempting to persuade;
expressing enthusiasm; bidding for attention;
scolding
Lifeskills Extensions:
comparing furniture prices; planning furniture
needs; planning purchasing priorities
Further Language Development:
vocabulary lists (furniture, appliances,
fixtures); writing about the picture;
student-directed true/false exercise

Picture 20: The Credit Office of a Furniture Store **82**

Differences
Context Questions
Language Functions:
urging; hedging; asking for clarification;
deliberately giving an unclear or confusing response
Lifeskills Extension and Language Development:
scrambled story on making/breaking a contract
Further Language Development:
"I want" discussion/grammar/writing exercise;
pronunciation practice: initial/medial/final l or r;
discussion question

Picture 21: School Registration **86**

Differences
Context Questions
Language Functions:
directing a familiar; expressing impatience;
requesting routine service in a business
transaction; responding to a request for routine
service; asking for a stranger's attention/making
a reasonable request; asking for a co-worker's
attention/making a reasonable request; expressing
enthusiasm; bidding to join in the action
Lifeskills Extensions:
teaching how to communicate with local schools
Further Language Development:
cloze dictation exercise; listening comprehension
exercises (listen and write/draw)

Picture 22: A Parent-Teacher Conference **90**
> *Differences*
> *Context Questions*
> *Language Functions*:
>> giving a favorable report; giving an unfavorable
>> report with positive emphasis; asking for
>> clarification; giving clarification; calling
>> for attention; refusing attention
> *Lifeskills Extensions*:
>> using math in analysis and decision-making
> *Further Language Development*:
>> adjectives activity; reading and responding
>> to a letter from school; pronunciation and
>> listening discrimination: vowel sounds of
>> Standard American English

Additional Language Development Exercises **95**

Appendices

1. Incorporating Lifeskills Content **101**
2. Related Materials for Expanding Lifeskills Content **102**
3. CASAS* Lifeskills competencies, *LOOK AGAIN PICTURES*,
   and Related Materials **104**
4. Using American Names **109**
5. Information Gap Activities **109**
6. Using Overhead Projectors and Transparencies **110**
7. A Short List of Handy ESL References **111**

---

*CASAS is an acronym for *California Adult Student Assessment System*.

Table of Activities and Exercises for Language Development

Activities/Exercises	Pictures	Pages
Pronunciation		
Discrimination		
final -s/-es	3	95
final -ed	4	95
intonation of Yes/No questions	5*	25
contrasting intonation of Yes/No, What/How, and "Or" questions	16*	69
initial, medial, and final l and r	20	85
vowels	22	94
Listening Comprehension		
price checking	7	33
picture grids	7	33
TPR sequences	12	53
true/false listening comprehension	15	65
student-monitored dictations	16	69
listening comprehension to match statements to A, B, AB	16	97
listening comprehension to determine time of a statement	18	77
true/false exercise	19*	81
cloze dictation	21*	89
listen and write/draw exercises	21	89
Speaking		
Dialogs		
dialog development	3	17
dialog development through paraphrase	8	95
four-by-four dialogs	10*	45
character-dialog matching	14*	61
Teacher-student communication		
context questions	all pictures	
lifeskills discussion	most pictures	
grammar exercises	many pictures	
Student-student communication		
Collaboration:		
scrambled sentences	1*	9
cloze exercise	2*	13
dialog development through paraphrase	8	95

*duplicatable exercise included

Activities/Exercises	Pictures	Pages
Collabration, cont.:		
categorizing	8, 19	37, 81
matching exercises	9, 13, 14	41, 57, 61
vocabulary lists	10, 15, 19	45, 65, 81
Interaction:		
teacher-guided student questions	6	26
picture grids	7	33
true/false exercise	19*	81
"I want" exercise	20	85

Reading

scrambled sentences	1*, 5	9, 95
cloze exercises	2*	13
comparison shopping	7*, 19	33, 81
applying for a supermarket check-cashing card	8*	37
categorizing exercises	8, 19	37, 81
matching exercises	9*, 13, 14*	41, 57, 61
reading and filling out a deposit slip	13*	57
scrambled story	20*	82
reading and responding to a letter from school	22*	93

Writing

structured writing	most exercises	
controlled composition	3*	17
writing a letter of complaint	12*	53
writing a letter to a friend	15*	65
dictations	16, 21*	69, 89
writing about the picture	19	81
"I want" exercise	20	85
reading and responding to a letter from school	22*	93

Grammar-specific

"What <u>would</u> you like?" vs. "What <u>do</u> you like?"	1	9
third-person plural to third-person singular	3*	17
<u>too</u> vs. <u>enough</u>	4	21
passive voice	4*	21
simple present and frequency adverbs	5	95
understanding pronouns and making <u>Yes/No</u> questions	5*	25
adjective placement before nouns	6*	29
<u>-ed</u> vs. <u>-ing</u> adjectives	6	29

*duplicatable exercise included

Activities/Exercises	Pictures	Pages
modal auxiliary verbs	6	29
quantifiers	8	37
WH– questions	11*	49
contrast of "wish" and "hope"	13	96
future	15	65
past	15	65, 96
present perfect	15	96
"if" and unreal conditional	15	96
regular and irregular verbs	15	65
answers to Yes/No, WH–, and "Or" questions	16*	69
adjectives and adverbs of increase/decrease	17	73
using connectives: and, but, because, and so	17*	73
listening comprehension exercise to determine time	18	77
review of relative clause types	18*	77
"I want" exercise	20	85
comparative adjectives	all pictures	
there isn't/there aren't	all pictures	
doesn't/don't have	all pictures	
relative clauses	all pictures	
adjectives and adjectival prepositional phrases	all pictures	

Vocabulary-specific

-ed vs. -ing adjectives	6	29
picture grids	7	33
matching exercise for vocabulary development	9	41
building maintenance vocabulary	11	49
vocabulary lists	10, 15, 19	45, 65, 81
comparatives of size	17	73
nouns used as modifiers	17	97

Methods and techniques

scrambled sentences and stories	1*, 5, 20*	9, 95, 82
cloze exercises and cloze dictations	2*, 21*	13, 89
story problems	2, 3, 5, 6, 11, 15, 22	13, 17, 25, 29, 49, 65, 93
controlled composition	3	17
dialogs	3, 8, 10*, 14	17, 95, 45, 61
pattern drills	5	25
teacher-guided student questions	6	26
picture grids	7	33
listening comprehension exercises	7, 15, 16, 18, 19*, 21	33, 65, 69, 97, 77, 81, 89
categorizing	8, 19	37, 81

*duplicatable exercise included

Table of Activities and Exercises for Language Development

Activities/Exercises	Pictures	Pages
matching exercises	9*, 13, 14*	41, 57, 61
TPR sequences	12	53
true/false exercises	15, 19*	65, 81
dictations	16, 21*	69, 89

*duplicatable exercise included

Introduction

LOOK AGAIN PICTURES: What It Is and Who It's For

As a language teacher, I like problem-solving activities that involve my students in the material at hand. I like activities that inspire my students to talk or to be creative in their writing. I particularly like working with pictures that have enough content to let me come back to them again and again and find new ways of developing language exercises from them. For me, teaching is most rewarding when the material I am using gives me "nuggets" to teach from, and allows me enough flexibility to make up my own variations.

LOOK AGAIN PICTURES has been created to encourage the kinds of things I like doing. The pictures and exercises are intended for teacher use with high school and adult students at all levels of language development. They also may be used by teacher trainers and trainees. The picture units are not presented in any particular order. You may choose whichever ones suit your classroom needs.

Each of the twenty-two picture-pairs contains eight differences between the top and bottom pictures. The problem-solving activity asks students to compare the pictures and look for the differences—a variation on an old theme that has engaged people of all ages for centuries.

Hunting for the differences stimulates classroom discussion, and can be used as an activity for pairs or for small groups. Once students have found the differences, they have a real desire to communicate them to other members of the class and to the teacher.

Communicating this way helps students to interact with and to develop a personal relationship with the pictures and their content. There are various ways to build on this involvement, many of which are described in this book.

There is something else here, too: a potential for *you* to interact with the material, as well. LOOK AGAIN PICTURES is a sourcebook: it offers suggestions for developing language skills and lifeskills content through use of optional exercises that focus on vocabulary, grammar, language functions, problem solving, listening, speaking, pronunciation, reading, writing, and combinations of all these skills. You can decide what is most appropriate for the class (depending on the students' experiences, needs, and mood), and develop lessons accordingly.

When used by teacher trainers, the suggestions for each picture-page can become springboards for trainee assignments. Trainees can use LOOK AGAIN PICTURES to develop lessons using dialogs, grammar or pronunciation drills, listening exercises, and so on.

The picture-pages are designed to be removed from the book and used as blackline masters for student copies and for making overhead transparencies. Duplicatable exercises also appear on the back of each picture-page. All pictures are accompanied by text that includes:

- a list of the eight *Differences* between the pictures;
- *Context Questions* about the pictures;
- *Language Functions* appropriate to the interactions depicted in the pictures;
- *Lifeskills Extensions* activities and exercises appropriate to the pictures; and
- *Further Language Development* exercises.

How to Use LOOK AGAIN PICTURES Most Effectively

Finding the differences

The picture-pages have been designed to elicit from students certain kinds of grammatical forms describing the differences in the pictures. The most frequently used forms are: "There isn't/aren't, and X doesn't/don't have Y," to express the absence of something, and "-er, more, or less" to express comparison. *Adjectives, prepositional phrases,* and *relative clauses used as modifiers* indicate which character in a picture is different, such as "The tired old woman with the shopping basket" and "The man who is pointing to the sign." (*Picture 6: Riding on the Bus*, p. 26.)

The *bottom* picture on each picture-page will contain some differences designed to elicit the most frequently used forms. Other differences will elicit a variety of grammatical forms that tend to be used less frequently. One such difference that appears in many pictures is the change of direction in the placement or movement of a character, which is designed to elicit the phrase, "the other way."

The eight differences between the top and bottom pictures are identified in the *Differences* section of the text for each picture-page. Most of the differences are fairly subtle, so the challenge of finding them is a real one. Students become involved in making their discoveries and communicating what they have found to the rest of the class.

One reason for focusing on specific grammatical forms is that many students have problems using them correctly in natural communication. Repeated use of the pictures will give students practice in using the forms, while giving you an opportunity to assess student progress.

Procedure

1. Using the picture-page as a master, make photocopies for your students. If possible, make an overhead transparency too. (See *Appendix 6*, p. 110, for suggestions.)

2. Put students in pairs and give only one copy of a picture-page to each pair. This makes finding the differences a collaborative task. It's best if the partners do not have the same native language, so that they must communicate in English.

   However, if it isn't possible to find partners who speak different languages, it is still better to encourage students to work in pairs at this point. After the partners have found the eight differences between the pictures, they can collaborate on making good English sentences to express the differences. (After students have located the differences, give them the remaining copies of the picture-pages so that every student has a copy.)

3. Lead the class in a discussion of the differences, focusing students on the *bottom* picture as a point of reference. Use a projected transparency, if you have one. Have the students tell you the differences, using just a word or short phrase. List these differences on the board. Then expand the list by eliciting more details from students and forming complete, grammatical sentences at the appropriate level of complexity for your class.

Very beginning classes

If your students are not ready to handle comparatives and the other grammatical forms listed on p. 1, they can still participate in the picture-comparison discussion by using two basic patterns and pointing to the differences in the pictures: "This/That/These/Those is/are missing or This/That/These/Those is/are different." If students possess the vocabulary for describing the differences, they will undoubtedly use it. However, the two patterns make it possible for students to talk about the pictures without having to *name* the actual differences.

If you want the students to work on naming the differences, start by asking whether anyone knows the word for _____ . Let the students themselves provide as much of the vocabulary as possible.

At the very beginning level, you probably will want to use finding the differences mainly to develop vocabulary, focusing on frequently used words and on certain words that are different. For example, in *Picture 10: Talking to the Doctor*, p. 42, you may decide to identify the thermometer for vocabulary and pronunciation practice, but probably not the doctor's stethoscope (unless a student specifically asks about it). This is because students will need to recognize and talk about thermometers outside the classroom, on occasion, but probably will not need such familiarity with stethoscopes. The stethoscope is in the picture primarily to help the student identify the character as a doctor or other medical person.

High beginning–low intermediate classes

At this level, students should be exposed to "There isn't/aren't, -er, and more," and the placement of simple modifiers such as adjectives and prepositional phrases.

You may want to begin by discussing the differences to informally assess how much students can already produce, and then introduce a more structured grammar lesson based on the pictures. Or you could use the pictures for communication practice, following a formal lesson on adjectives and prepositional phrases as modifiers.

Intermediate classes

Many students at this level will have a general sense of the grammatical forms, "There isn't/aren't," but still need more practice to avoid saying such things as "There no have..."

At the intermediate level, students should have mastered the placement of adjectives and modifying prepositional phrases fairly well, and should be working with relative clauses and reduced relative clauses, such as "The man who is looking at his watch," or "The man looking at his watch." (*Picture 4: Exchanges and Layaways*, p. 18.)

Advanced classes

At this level, the students should be familiar with most of the grammatical forms and the vocabulary, although these may be imperfectly mastered in oral production.

An appropriate challenge for this level might be to have students express each of the eight differences in three different ways, for a total of twenty-four sentences. For another challenge, ask students to create the longest grammatical sentence possible to express each difference, for a total of eight sentences. Encourage students to collaborate and compete in teams. Such activities are good stimuli for student questions that begin with "Can I say it this way: _____ ?"

Whatever level class you are teaching, you will find that students have a certain natural interest in finding the differences, and in communicating what they are. The activity can move quickly or slowly, depending on the level of the class and on how thorough you want to be.

After having the students find and discuss the differences, and perhaps write them down, you may want to stop. But there is much more that can be done with *LOOK AGAIN PICTURES*.

Discussing the context

Some teachers like to discuss picture context before comparing picture-pairs to find the differences. Others prefer to compare the pictures first. You can proceed either way. You may want to experiment, starting with comparison on some pictures and with discussion of context on others.

In beginning with a discussion of the context, you will find it helpful to tell students to fold their papers so that just one picture is showing—top or bottom. The *Context Questions* section of each picture-page text will tell you which picture to use for this activity.

You will also find it useful to use a transparency of the pictures on an overhead projector (see Appendix 6, p. 110) and to mask one of the pictures while you discuss the other. (You also may want to mask the picture title if you ask the context question, "<u>Where</u> are these people?") Using a projected transparency lets you point easily to parts of the picture, and facilitates discussion.

The *Context Questions* list general, *suggested* questions about the picture context. Many are open-ended, with no one right answer, to encourage student thinking and involvement. Frequently, there are clues within the pictures that make some answers more appropriate than others. These clues encourage attention to detail and help students develop interpretive thinking skills.

Using the given *Context Questions* (or others you have created) will encourage students to help you develop stories that can become the basis for further language development exercises. Student ideas that are incorporated into the story will help the story become more "theirs" and may incidentally give you some ideas you hadn't thought of.

Student answers will also help you assess how much language your students can produce accurately when their attention is on communication rather than on form. Their answers may also give you ideas for grammar and pronunciation points to present or review.

However, keep in mind that when students are telling you about the picture for the first time, their focus on communication is likely to result in less control of grammatical forms. Don't press for accuracy the first time around if it is not forthcoming. The business of communicating may be enough of a task. For work on grammatical accuracy, ask the *Context Questions* again later, when the picture is more familiar.

During your discussion, try referring to characters by number or by name. Projecting an overhead transparency of the picture will facilitate discussion, as you can write the name or numbers right on the characters themselves.

In naming your characters, avoid overuse of common American names, such as John, Bill, and Mary. Choose names that may be less familiar to your students, such as Karen, Phil, Jan, or names that present pronunciation difficulties, as in the list shown in *Picture 22: A Parent-Teacher Conference*, p. 90. A list of male and female names on the wall for a semester's practice will facilitate on-the-spot naming: You and the students can choose names from the list. You might want to include your students' names, as well. (See *Appendix 4*, p. 109, for further suggestions.)

Not using names at all is one way to make your discussion of context more challenging. This encourages students to use different grammatical forms, such as prepositional phrases and relative clauses, to describe the many characters in the pictures.

In lower-level classes, student responses may encourage you to do a lesson on adjective placement, such as "the big angry man" or "the tired old woman," or to do a lesson on use of the phrase <u>with</u> + noun as in "the man with the glasses" or "the person with the cigarette." (See *Picture 5: Getting on the Bus*, p. 22.)

In more advanced classes, discussion might lead to a lesson or review of relative clauses and participial adjectives, as in, "the man who is pointing to a boiling pot." (See *Picture 2: A Coffee Shop Kitchen*, p. 10.)

When beginning students talk about the pictures, they can, of course, resort to saying "he" and "she" or "that man" and "that woman," while pointing. But you can encourage students who are beyond the beginning level to produce more. For example, if you ask, "Which man?" and the student responds, "The man with the glasses," then you can request more detail: "But there are *three* men wearing glasses. *Which* man? Give me more details."

In my intermediate and advanced classes, I sometimes find it useful to push students to grope for new ways to describe the character or item they have in mind. A few moments of confusion are acceptable; during this time, a student may remember a word or form s/he has heard before and try to apply it to this new context.

If, after a period of groping, the students do not produce an answer, then I provide it. Later I teach a lesson on that word or grammatical form. In a subsequent discussion, students describe the picture again, trying to use the new expression without referring to their notes from the lesson.

Occasionally, using the picture as a challenge to practice new words and grammatical forms can be an interesting alternative to the "safe" practice of familiar language that the student has already mastered.

As teacher, you are in the best position to know how much less-than-accurate-but-still-informative communication to accept from any particular student, and how much to push for more detail or accuracy. Keep in mind the multiple purposes of discussing the context:

- getting students involved with the picture and lifeskills subject matter;
- assessing their communication skills and mastery of grammatical form while communicating; and
- getting ideas for follow-up grammar and pronunciation lessons, role plays, reading, and writing exercises.

By the way, the assessment step is a good activity for Fridays: It gives you the weekend to plan what kind of follow-up you would like to do.

You will find *suggested* activities and exercises throughout the book in the *Lifeskills Extensions* and *Further Language Development* sections of each picture-page text. Many of these suggestions will no doubt need adjustment to fit the level and needs of your class. My intent is to give you ideas for a variety of lessons that you can develop to expand the context of the pictures you choose to use. Lesson ideas that go with one picture often can be modified to fit several other pictures as well.

Language functions

In many language classes, an interesting picture will lead to classroom interaction *about* the picture—generally with students recounting, listing, and describing aspects of the picture in response to questions.

BUT in the world outside the classroom, people must interact in a number of different ways that may receive scant attention in the classroom: *apologizing, bantering, congratulating, demanding, empathizing, flattering*, and so on.

These are some of the things that people must *do* with the language in everyday encounters. They are often referred to as language functions.

In *LOOK AGAIN PICTURES*, many kinds of lifeskills interactions are depicted to provide settings for practicing different ways of using English outside the classroom. The *Language Functions* text for each picture-page lists some of the language functions that the interactions are intended to depict. You may think of others, as well. Accompanying each language function are possible statements to express it. These statements are *suggestions*—they are provided to get you thinking. You will decide what language is most appropriate to use with your students.

The language to express the indicated functions can be presented in straightforward dialog or in dialog variations, such as scrambled dialogs (p. 17), four-by-four dialogs (p. 45), or exercises matching utterances to characters (p. 61).

In order for students to develop any real proficiency with particular functions in specific situations, they will need more than one practice session. In successive classes, you can move toward freer role play of these situations, letting students use their own words.

Before introducing any dialogs or role plays, assess your students. Elicit statements about the characters in the picture via questions like these: "What do you think s/he is (they are) saying?" or "If you were this person, what would you say?" The statements will give you an idea of what your students are already familiar with, and may also give you some words and phrases to incorporate or to build on as you develop activities to go with the pictures.

In preparing dialogs or monitoring role plays, pay attention to the appropriateness of the language with respect to the following considerations:

1. *The type of situation* being depicted, and *the relationship of the characters*. For instance, the language that is used to persuade people to make a $25 purchase may not sound the same as the language used to persuade them to make a $900 purchase; apologizing to a stranger may be different from apologizing to a friend; and so on.

2. *The identity of characters* in the pictures and *of your students*. Listen to people around you who are similar to the characters in the picture. What do they *really* say? Incorporate their speech into your lesson when possible.

   Two factors that influence a person's language in subtle ways are sex and age. For instance, the language used by an eighteen-year-old woman is often somewhat different from the language of, say, a forty-year-old man in the same situation.

   When you prepare dialogs for picture characters that represent speech of the opposite sex, check with colleagues of that sex for appropriateness of language. If the character is much older or younger than you are, check with someone nearer the age of that character: "If you were this person in this situation, what would you say?" But when your students roleplay any situation, take care that the language they use is appropriate for their own age and sex—that is, they should roleplay *themselves* in the situation whenever possible.

3. Another consideration in developing appropriate language is *regional location*. People in different parts of the country have somewhat different ways

of expressing themselves. This is why you are encouraged to develop your own dialogs, rather than rely on published material.

In the end, of course, there must be a balance between appropriateness of language and your students' ability to handle the level of that language. As teacher, you can best decide what that balance will be.

It is well to remember, however, that in "real life" interactions, people more readily overlook imperfect grammar than they do the wrong tone or manner, or words perceived as too forceful in a delicate situation.

Lifeskills extensions

Competency-based lifeskills programs have become a major component of adult and high school curricula in California and many other states. The California Adult Student Assessment System (CASAS) has developed a set of objective statements concerning specific competencies that adults should be able to demonstrate in various lifeskills.

Appendix 3, pp. 104–08, gives more information about the CASAS competencies to which *LOOK AGAIN PICTURES* relates directly or indirectly. Also included is a list of published materials containing a variety of appropriate exercises for developing these competencies.

The *Lifeskills Extensions* text for each picture-page refers to this appendix and also provides *suggested* lifeskills activities to accompany the picture. While *LOOK AGAIN PICTURES* does not teach lifeskills, the *Lifeskills Extensions* provide a context in which lifeskills material can be introduced. A general pictorial context is particularly helpful for introducing lifeskills in beginning classes. For instance, *Picture 13: A Bank Line* and *Picture 14: A Bank Desk*, on pp. 54 and 58, respec-

tively, will help set the stage for exercises using checks or bank account applications. *Picture 9: A Clinic Waiting Room* and *Picture 10: Talking to the Doctor*, on pp. 38 and 42, respectively, can precede activities such as reading and discussing prescription instructions or dosage information on medicine containers, or giving verbal health histories.

Further language development

LOOK AGAIN PICTURES can stimulate other kinds of language practice besides discussions of picture differences, function-based dialogs, and lifeskills interaction. The pictures may also provide stimuli for writing exercises, contexts for listening exercises, or subject matter for vocabulary, pronunciation, and grammar exercises.

The *Further Language Development* sections for many of the picture-page texts contain *sample* grammar-oriented activities and exercises. Keep in mind that these are prototypes: They may be suitable for adaptation to other pictures as well. For most pictures, a language development exercise is presented in a duplicatable format on the back of the picture-page, and may be copied for classroom use. See asterisked entries in the Table of Activities and Exercises for Language Development (following the Table of Contents).

As you work with the pictures, you will discover ways to relate them to whatever grammar your class may be studying. Have your students use the pictures as a springboard for "creative practice." Encourage them to make up sentences about the pictures using whatever grammatical form(s) they have been studying or already know.

And when you're absolutely *sure* you've exhausted all the possibilities—remember to "look again"!

1 A Coffee Shop

Class discussion resulting from such questions will give you a chance to informally assess actual student performance in various language skills and lifeskills, with an eye to developing appropriate follow-up materials for the picture. (See pp. 3–4 for more details.)

FOLD PAPERS TO LOOK AT THE *BOTTOM* PICTURE ONLY.
- Where are these people? Do you think it's very expensive to eat there? Why do you think so?
- What time of day is it? Why do you think so?
- What has just happened in the booth?
- What is just about to happen at the counter?
- Who are the people in the picture? Describe them and give them names.
- What was each of these people doing one half hour ago? (Make a guess; use your imagination.)
- What will each of them be doing one half hour from now? (Make a guess; use your imagination.)

Differences

(Circled in *bottom* picture, left to right)

1. menu larger, or more items   2. hair curly
3. straw the other way   4. sleeve shorter
5. frowning instead of smiling   6. less hair, or balder   7. boots instead of shoes (*Note*: Pronunciation contrast of <u>boots</u> vs. <u>booth</u>)
8. no belt

STUDENTS SHOULD DESCRIBE CHANGES IN *BOTTOM* PICTURE. See pp. 1–3 for suggestions on implementation in beginning, intermediate, and advanced classes.

Context Questions

Let students participate with you in creating a story from this picture. Many of the questions below are open-ended—there is no one right answer—in order to encourage student involvement. Some questions depend on interpretation of clues within the picture, to encourage active thinking and attention to detail.

All questions are intended as guides only. You may think of other ways of phrasing them for your students. Or you may think of other questions.

Language Functions

Language functions describe what people *do* with the language when they interact with each other.

Through structured dialogs, dialog development activities, and creative role play, we can give our students practice using the language in these different ways in situations that are important for their lives. Check the Table of Activities and Exercises for Language Development (following the Table of Contents), for dialog activities found in this book.

Some functions appropriate to this picture are listed below. You may think of others. The examples given for each function are intended to stimulate your thinking. Reword them as necessary to fit your region of the country, the abilities of your students, and your particular lesson. (See pp. 4–5 for more details.)

Taking an order: "Are you ready to order?/What would you like today?...What would you like with that?...How would you like it cooked?...Anything else?...For here or to go?/To take out?"

Ordering: "No, not yet...Yes, I'd like/I'll have a/some...How's the _____?...That's all...To go, please."

Expressing displeased surprise: "Hey!...Watch out!/Look out!...Be careful!"

Expressing surprise/apologizing: "Oops...Hey, I'm really sorry...Boy, am I clumsy!...Whoops, excuse, please."

Extension: How do our apologies differ when extended to a close friend? to a stranger? to an older or younger person? if our error is minor or severe? if the error was avoidable or unavoidable?

1
A Coffee Shop

Can you find EIGHT differences between these pictures?

Scrambled Sentences

The words in these sentences are mixed up. Use the same words to write good sentences that tell about the picture.

1. ? coffee with you friends go your ever to Do shops

_____

2. . Jack's between teenagers These to like classes Shop to Coffee go

_____

_____

3. . drinking yesterday and They sodas were there , talking

_____

4. . at Another ordering the was something to eat counter person sitting and

_____

_____

5. ? get or Did hamburger she sandwich a a

_____

6. . remember She doesn't what ordered she

_____

7. . wasn't about food She thinking the ; about was owner thinking the she

_____

_____

8. . , , likes too and him her likes he She

_____

9. . comes on frequently She break here her

_____

10. ? him Will someday marry ask he to her

_____

After you answer question 10, write a dialog between the people at the counter.

_____

8

Lifeskills Extensions

See *Appendix 3*, pp. 104–08, for a list of specific likeskills competencies and published materials that suggest activities appropriate for this picture context.

Ordering from a menu: For intermediate or advanced students, copy an actual coffee shop menu. For beginning students, develop a simplified menu, using some items that students already know and a few new ones.

The first day that you use *Picture 1*, find out how many menu items your students are familiar with. Arrange the students into small groups; have them list items of food and drink that might be ordered in a coffee shop or restaurant. The groups can then read their lists to the rest of the class while you record the items on the board.

Getting a sense of how much your students already know will help you decide how detailed a menu to present to them. In your lesson, don't forget to include at least some of the choices Americans are faced with when ordering:

- **eggs**: sunny side up? over easy? scrambled? soft-boiled?
- **meat**: rare? medium? well done?
- **salad**: with French, Italian, Russian, Roquefort dressing?

All items and choices will, of course, be determined by what is available in your local coffee shops.

Checking the bill/figuring the tip: Duplicate a real restaurant bill, and have students examine it for accuracy. Is the total correct? If there is a state sales tax, was it computed correctly? How much tip should be left?

To develop students' listening comprehension, collect and duplicate several restaurant or coffee shop bills on one page. Distribute these pages to your students. Then describe what someone ordered, and have students listen without looking at the bills while you are talking. Then ask the students to choose the appropriate bill.

Or take the role of a customer and give an order for students to write down. Have them figure the tax. You can also tape-record different people with different speaking styles giving orders, and have the students take these orders down.

Further Language Development

What would you like? vs. What do you like?: Using this picture context, explore the difference between "What would you like?" and "What do you like?" which students often confuse.

Scrambled sentences: In a high-beginning or low-intermediate class, use the duplicatable scrambled sentence exercise on the back of *Picture 1* to help students develop a sense of word order. Or develop something similar to fit the needs and level of your class.

Pair students and give one copy of the exercise to each pair. Have pairs work together. When they are finished, have them compare their work with that of other pairs.

Review the exercise with the class, and discuss the last question. Then ask students to write the dialog called for at the end of the exercise, to be shared with the other students in a later class.

Answer Key

1. Do you ever go to coffee shops with your friends?
2. These teenagers like to go to Jack's Coffee Shop between classes.
3. They were there yesterday, drinking sodas and talking.
4. Another person was sitting at the counter and ordering something to eat.
5. Did she get a hamburger or a sandwich?
6. She doesn't remember what she ordered.
7. She wasn't thinking about the food; she was thinking about the owner.
8. She likes him, and he likes her, too.
9. She comes here frequently on her break.
10. Will he ask her to marry him someday?

2 A Coffee Shop Kitchen

Differences

(Circled in *bottom* picture, left to right)

1. apron shorter **2.** fewer plates **3.** no stripes, or no pattern **4.** pan smaller **5.** apron cleaner **6.** face cleaner, or doesn't need a shave **7.** no ad circled in newspaper **8.** no checks, or plaid, or pattern

STUDENTS SHOULD DESCRIBE CHANGES IN *BOTTOM* PICTURE. See pp. 1–3 for suggestions on implementation in beginning, intermediate, and advanced classes.

Context Questions

Let students participate with you in creating a story from this picture. Many of the questions below are open-ended—there is no one right answer—in order to encourage student involvement. Some questions depend on interpretation of clues within the picture, to encourage active thinking and attention to detail.

All questions are intended as guides only. You may think of other ways of phrasing them for your students. Or you may think of other questions.

Class discussion resulting from such questions will give you a chance to informally assess actual student performance in various language skills and lifeskills, with an eye to developing appropriate follow-up materials for the picture. (See pp. 3–4 for more details.)

FOLD PAPERS TO LOOK AT THE *TOP* PICTURE ONLY.
- Where are these people? Why do you think so?
- What time of day is it? Why do you think so?
- Who is the large man in the dirty apron? Who is the young man who isn't wearing an apron? What are they doing? Why do you think so?
- What has just happened at the stove? What's going to happen next?
- Would you like to work there? Why or why not?

Language Functions

Language functions describe what people *do* with the language when they interact with each other.

Through structured dialogs, dialog development activities, and creative role play, we can give our students practice using the language in these different ways in situations that are important for their lives. Check the Table of Activities and Exercises for Language Development (following the Table of Contents), for dialog activities found in this book.

Some functions appropriate to this picture are listed below. You may think of others. The examples given for each function are intended to stimulate your thinking. Reword them as necessary to fit your region of the country, the abilities of your students, and your particular lesson. (See pp. 4–5 for more details.)

Exclaiming and warning: "Hey, watch out! Look out! Be careful! Hey, look! Hey, _____!"

Responding to a warning: "Huh? Oh, thanks . . . Oops, thanks . . . Right . . . Got it."

Asking for specific job information: "I saw this ad in the paper . . . Are you still looking for someone? What are the hours? What is the pay? What do I have to do?"

Giving specific job information: "You've got to . . . We need somebody who . . ."

Asking about job experience: "Have you ever done this kind of work before? Have you ever worked before? Where? When? What did you do? What can you do?"

Giving job experience: "Yeah, I worked in my uncle's cafe in Da Nang . . . No, but my welfare got cut off and I really need to find something . . ."

2
A Coffee Shop Kitchen

Can you find EIGHT differences between these pictures?

NAME _____ CLASS _____

Using Prepositions

Please fill in the blanks below with the following words. Some words are used more than once.

| about | of | on | to |
| for | off | out | up |

     Look at this kitchen. All kinds _____ things are going on. _____ the stove, a
        (1)   (2)

pot has just boiled _____, but the cook's helper isn't paying any attention _____it.
             (3)   (4)

He's busy working _____ something else. The dishwasher is trying to warn him
            (5)

_____ it. He's afraid that he's going to have to wipe _____ the mess after the
  (6)   (7)

helper turns _____ the burner.
       (8)

     Something else is going _____ at the door. There's an eager young applicant
                  (9)

_____ a job. He hasn't had much experience, but he looks like he'll be easy _____
 (10)   (11)

train. The boss is looking him _____. He needs more help right away, but he wants to
                  (12)

find _____ more about the young man before offering him the job. The last new helper
    (13)

they had didn't work _____ at all. They had to let him go after only two days.
            (14)

12

Lifeskills Extensions

See *Appendix 3*, pp. 104–08, for a list of specific lifeskills competencies and published materials that suggest activities appropriate for this picture context.

"Help Wanted" ads: For intermediate and advanced students, bring in ads from local newspapers and discuss the abbreviations. Create a matching exercise by putting the abbreviations in one column and explanations of those abbreviations in another column for students to match.

Story problems: Duplicate a page of "Help Wanted" ads from the local newspaper. Write and duplicate story problems for reading or listening comprehension. Distribute the ads and problems to your students.

Example

Juan is looking for a night job so that he can go to school in the afternoon. He has twelve years' experience as a mechanic in his country, and six months' experience as a dishwasher in the U.S. He doesn't want to do any more dishwashing.

Read the ads and then list three businesses where Juan might apply for a job.

The story problems should be at the level of language that is appropriate for your students, and should relate as closely as possible to actual ads you show them. In reviewing the ads, discuss the probable behavior, dress, and requirements of different kinds of jobs and job sites such as a large company office vs. a small coffee shop.

Job application forms: Identify local firms that offer jobs your upper beginning and intermediate students are likely to apply for. Obtain and duplicate job-application forms from these firms. Distribute and discuss the forms in class, giving students a chance to talk with you about the jobs each firm might have available, and to read, question, and use the vocabulary on the forms. Students can practice gathering the information they need to fill out the forms before actually completing the applications. If actual job openings exist, encourage qualified students to try their new job-application skills in the workplace.

Workers' rights: Obtain a minimum wage information poster from your local office of the U.S. Department of Labor, an unemployment insurance information poster from the State Department of Employment, and a posting copy of the State Department of Labor Relations standards for health and safety on the job. Develop dialog and story-problem exercises designed to help your beginning and intermediate students learn their workplace rights under federal and state laws.

Further Language Development

Cloze exercises

Language teachers have adapted the cloze technique in many ways to focus on various aspects of reading comprehension, grammar and usage, and vocabulary. A traditional cloze exercise is prepared by taking a reading passage and deleting every *nth* word, often every seventh or ninth word. If the passage is written at a controlled language level, readers at that level should be able to deduce enough from the context to fill in at least 80 percent of the blanks. To make the exercise more difficult, use a more advanced language level and/or delete more words; to make the exercise less difficult, use a less advanced language level and/or delete fewer words.

Procedure: You can prepare a cloze exercise ahead of time and duplicate it for your students for individual or small-group work, or you can write it spontaneously on the board for the class to read together. After students have completed the blackboard cloze the first time by telling you what to write in the blanks, erase different parts of the passage and have the students do it again. The advantage of writing a cloze exercise on the board is that you can present it spontaneously and control it closely.

You can also present a duplicated or blackboard cloze exercise as a dictation. Read the passage at normal speed and have students fill in the blanks as they listen. For a blackboard cloze, students write only the deleted words on a separate piece of paper. If the text is challenging, reading it aloud will not give away the answers.

Another possibility is to make a cloze a small-group collaborative exercise. This approach encourages peer teaching and discussion about English (even *in English*, if your students have different language backgrounds).

The duplicatable cloze exercise on the back of *Picture 2* was prepared for an intermediate adult school class that was learning prepositions. It may give you ideas for similar exercises appropriate to the needs and level of your class. Because the deleted matter concerned usages that may be unfamiliar to some students, the answers are given at the bottom of the sheet.

③ A Clothing Sale

Differences

(Circled in *bottom* picture, left to right)

1. fewer bags **2.** woman larger or heavier ("Fatter" does not really apply here. "Large" and "heavy" are considered politer terms for describing a big person's size.) **3.** no tie **4.** sign different **5.** fewer suits **6.** sleeves rolled up **7.** arm higher **8.** more jacket buttons

STUDENTS SHOULD DESCRIBE CHANGES IN *BOTTOM* PICTURE. See pp. 1–3 for suggestions on implementation in beginning, intermediate, and advanced classes.

Context Questions

Let students participate with you in creating a story from this picture. Many of the questions below are open-ended—there is no one right answer—in order to encourage student involvement. Some questions depend on interpretation of clues within the picture, to encourage active thinking and attention to detail.

All questions are intended as guides only. You may think of other ways of phrasing them for your students. Or you may think of other questions.

Class discussion resulting from such questions will give you a chance to informally assess actual student performance in various language skills and lifeskills, with an eye to developing appropriate follow-up materials for the picture. (See pp. 3–4 for more details.)

FOLD PAPERS TO LOOK AT THE *TOP* PICTURE ONLY.
- Where are these people? Why do you think so?
- Can you name some stores near here with departments like this one?
- Are all of the people customers? If not, who is and who isn't? Why do you think so?
- Have the customers been successful in finding what they need? Why do you think so?
- Look at the people's faces. How do they feel? Why do you think they feel that way? (The woman could be smiling with approval or in amusement; the man at the mirror could be confused or disappointed; the man holding the plaid pants could be puzzled or disappointed.)
- Who is the woman in the picture? (Possibly the wife, friend, or sister of the man at the mirror.)
- Some people in the picture are holding something; some are doing something. Who is each person and what is s/he holding or doing?
- As a class, give all the characters names, or have students refer to the characters by description, as in "The man who is kneeling . . ."

Language Functions

Language functions describe what people *do* with the language when they interact with each other.

Through structured dialogs, dialog development activities, and creative role play, we can give our students practice using the language in these different ways in situations that are important for their lives. Check the Table of Activities and Exercises for Language Development (following the Table of Contents), for dialog activities found in this book.

Some functions appropriate to this picture are listed below. You may think of others. The examples given for each function are intended to stimulate your thinking. Reword them as necessary to fit your region of the country, the abilities of your students, and your particular lesson. (See pp. 4–5 for more details.)

Asking for clarification: "Are you sure this will fit? . . . Are these the only ones on sale?"

Expressing doubt: "I'm not sure this is right for me/if these will fit . . . I don't know if I like this."

Hedging or polite put-offs: "Well . . . I don't know . . . Let me think about it . . ."

3
A Clothing Sale

Can you find EIGHT differences between these pictures?

Reading, Grammar, and Writing

Read the story below. Then read and follow the directions in the box under the story. If you don't understand some of the words, ask your teacher.

Mr. and Mrs. Lee often go shopping on weekends. They need nice clothes for their jobs, but they don't want to spend a lot of money, so they usually buy their clothes on sale.

Sometimes they look for a long time before they find something they like. They always watch the newspaper ads for sales, and they try to get to the stores early on a sale day.

Why do they save their money so carefully? Because they want to buy a house next year—or maybe the year after. When they have more money in the bank, they'll start looking at houses instead of clothes.

Directions:

1. Read the story aloud.

2. Find and underline the frequency adverbs: words like *always*, *usually*, and *sometimes*. What do they mean?

3. Write questions about the story, such as: "What do Mr. and Mrs. Lee often do on weekends?"

4. Rewrite the story, changing "Mr. and Mrs. Lee" to "Mr. Lee." You will also have to change all of the verbs and pronouns. Follow the original, but be careful to make all the changes. Your story should begin: "<u>Mr. Lee</u> often <u>goes</u> shopping on weekends. He needs nice clothes for <u>his job,</u> but . . . "

When you finish your writing, check it over very carefully and underline your changes before giving it to your teacher. You should have many changes from the original.

Expressing disapproval: "This is terrible...This isn't right for me at all...Don't you have anything smaller/larger?"

Reassuring: "Don't worry, sir. We have a good alterations department."

Expressing amusement/teasing: "Are you sure it's big enough, dear?"

Expressing approval: "That's a good color on you...That's good fabric."

Lifeskills Extensions

See *Appendix 3*, pp. 104–08, for a list of specific lifeskills competencies and published materials that suggest activities appropriate for this picture context.

Reading ads: Bring in clothing ads from newspapers for reading and discussion by your high-beginning, intermediate, and advanced students. Compare regular and sale prices to determine percent off, or apply a percentage discount to a regular price to determine what a sale price would be. Compare ads from different stores for similar items.

Contact assignment: Ask students who live, work, or travel near certain stores to check prices on one or two standard items in each store. Compare the prices in class.

Story problems for reading, computation, and discussion: Create story problems for your class at their language level. Include expressions such as "_____ % off," "marked down," "as is," and the like.

Example

Mrs. Kim went to a sale at Lacey's Department Store. She found men's slacks that regularly sell for $65 at 50% off. She also found slacks that regularly sell for $45 marked down to $29.95. She can buy only one pair of slacks for her husband.

Which one should she buy? What other things besides price should she consider?

Topics for class discussion: Talk about the times of year for certain kinds of sales; discount stores in the area; sales tax (if you have it) and what it is used for.

Further Language Development

Dialog activities
Dialogs appropriate to the level of your class can also be created from the picture.

For upper-beginning classes:
A. Do you like it?
B. It's much too big.
A. But we can alter it.
B. How much?

A. Only $10 more.
B. Well, I don't know...What do you think, dear?
C. You look pretty funny. You look like a little boy in his father's suit.
B. Okay, okay. Do you like the color?
C. Not really. Let's look at some other suits.
B. No, I'm tired of this. Let's go home.

For upper-intermediate classes:
A. Well, what do you think?
B. Are you sure it's big enough?
A. Quit joking, Myra. Do you like it or not? They can alter it, you know.
B. Well, it's 20% off, but that's still a lot of money. I don't think the color is very good on you.
A. Oh, okay. I'll take you out to dinner in my old suit, then.
B. Great! Then we'll have more money for a good time!

As additional accompanying activities, you might try the following:
- Read the dialog twice. Have students paraphrase it.
- Read the dialog and ask students to change it into reported speech. For example, "He asked her what she thought/if she liked the suit..."
- Read (or have students read) the dialog. Ask students to identify the speakers, their relationship, and their feelings. For example, "**B** seems to be teasing at first"; "**A** seems to be irritated," and the like.
- Prepare a cloze or scrambled sentences exercise using the dialog text. (If you decide on scrambled sentences, put the utterances out of sequence.)

Reading, grammar, and controlled composition
Use the duplicatable exercise on the back of *Picture 3* to provide high-beginning and intermediate students with practice in:
- reading;
- recognizing frequency adverbs;
- developing questions about reading matter; and
- changing verbs and pronouns in context from third-person plural to third-person singular through controlled composition.

Or develop something similar to fit the needs and level of your class.

Note: See *Additional Language Development Exercises*, pp. 95–97, for pronunciation practice to accompany this picture.

Picture 3: A Clothing Sale

17

4 Exchanges and Layaways

Differences

(Circled in *bottom* picture, left to right)

1. collar different   **2.** buttons or snaps instead of zipper   **3.** no beard   **4.** clock larger   **5.** hair shorter   **6.** time different   **7.** no flowers, or pattern, on skirt   **8.** toaster cord on the other side

STUDENTS SHOULD DESCRIBE CHANGES IN *BOTTOM* PICTURE. See pp. 1–3 for suggestions on implementation in beginning, intermediate, and advanced classes.

Context Questions

Let students participate with you in creating a story from this picture. Many of the questions below are open-ended—there is no one right answer— in order to encourage student involvement. Some questions depend on interpretation of clues within the picture, to encourage active thinking and attention to detail.

All questions are intended as guides only. You may think of other ways of phrasing them for your students. Or you may think of other questions.

Class discussion resulting from such questions will give you a chance to informally assess actual student performance in various language skills and lifeskills, with an eye to developing appropriate follow-up materials for the picture. (See pp. 3–4 for more details.)

FOLD PAPERS TO LOOK AT THE *TOP* PICTURE ONLY.
- Where are these people? Why do you think so?
- Why are they there? Why do you think so?
- Describe each person. What does s/he look like? How do you think each person feels?
- What is each person holding? Can you tell?
- Which people have something to exchange? Why do you think so?
- Why would a person want to exchange something? (Because it's broken/torn/damaged/too big/small/impractical/expensive.)
- Why would a person put something on layaway?
- Which people have something for layaway? Why do you think so?

Language Functions

Language functions describe what people *do* with the language when they interact with each other.

Through structured dialogs, dialog development activities, and creative role play, we can give our students practice using the language in these different ways in situations that are important for their lives. Check the Table of Activities and Exercises for Language Development (following the Table of Contents), for dialog activities found in this book.

Some functions appropriate to this picture are listed below. You may think of others. The examples given for each function are intended to stimulate your thinking. Reword them as necessary to fit your region of the country, the abilities of your students, and your particular lesson. (See pp. 4–5 for more details.)

Eliciting customer response: "Can I help you? ...Is this for exchange or layaway?...What seems to be the problem?/What's wrong with it?... Did you check it before you bought it?... Where's your receipt?" (*Note*: Students will need to comprehend this language more than they will need to produce it. You could roleplay the clerk, firing rapid questions at students; each student could roleplay a different customer in the picture.)

Making customer complaints about defects and malfunctions: "This _____ doesn't work. The cord/handle/lever is bent/broken...This/These _____ is/are too large/small...not large/small enough...the wrong size...This has a hole/tear/rip in it...The zipper is broken/hook is missing...It's stained..." and the like.

Look Again Pictures

4
Exchanges and Layaways

Can you find EIGHT differences between these pictures?

Using Passive Voice

Rewrite these sentences, changing the underlined phrases to the passive voice.

1. <u>Betsy needs to alter her dress</u> because it's too long in the waist.

   Betsy's dress needs to be altered because it's too long in the waist.

2. <u>Sam broke his new tennis racket</u> after only seven hours of play.

3. <u>Fred has to return his purchase</u> before the end of the month.

4. <u>They have to repair Lim's clock</u> while it's still under warranty.

5. <u>Carla will exchange the shoes</u> because they're too big.

6. <u>They have to fix Mrs. Lee's new toaster</u> because <u>someone damaged the cord</u> before she bought it.

Describing options: (On exchanges): "You can exchange it for another one, if you like. Otherwise, we can give you a credit receipt if you charged it, or a refund if you paid cash." (On layaways): "We have two plans. On one you pay _____ % down, and the balance plus tax in _____ days, with no service charge. On the other, you pay _____ % down, and the balance in two or more payments, including tax and service charge."

Asking for clarification of layaway terms: "How much deposit do I have to pay? What do I pay a month? What happens if I miss a payment? What's the total, with service charge?"

Lifeskills Extensions

See *Appendix 3*, pp. 104–08, for a list of specific lifeskills competencies and published materials that suggest activities appropriate for this picture context.

Exchanges and returns policies: Discuss the policies of different stores. (Most larger department stores will give credit or refund money, even on many sale items, *if the customer has a charge or cash receipt.* Many smaller stores will not take exchanges or returns on sale items or on items purchased more than a month earlier. Most stores will not give cash refunds on charged purchases and instead will give the customer credit against his/her outstanding balance. Check with the stores that your students are likely to frequent, or assign different students to check on the policies at stores they like.)

Comparing purchasing methods: Through story-problems that involve computation, compare the advantages and disadvantages of charge accounts with interest, layaways with service charges, and cash transactions.

Further Language Development

Too vs. enough

For beginning students, this would be a good exercise to practice:

Example

too small = not big enough
   His coat is too small.
   His coat is not big enough.
too big = not small enough
   His coat is too big.
   His coat is not small enough.

With upper-beginning students, you could use the blackboard to introduce the following pattern:

Example

(Name's) _____ doesn't/don't fit.
It's/They're too big/not small enough for him/her.
It's/They're too small/not big enough for him/her.

Use flashcards with pictures and/or words for clothing items, and draw stick figures of large and small people on the blackboard. Name the figures as you talk about them. For example, point to a small stick figure, hold up a card showing a sweater, and say, "Tell me about Fred." Students say, "Fred's sweater doesn't fit. It's too big for him." Or, "It's not small enough for him." (You can point to the pattern on the board.) Next, point to a large stick figure, hold up a card showing shoes, and say, "Tell me about Sally." Students say, "Sally's shoes don't fit. They're too small for her." The introductory or culminating activity can be naming the characters in the picture and talking about the fit of their clothes.

For intermediate and advanced classes, have students make six or more sentences using the words "too" and "enough." Possible phrases might include "too expensive," "not enough money/time/patience," and the like. More advanced classes may find it interesting to compare the forms not + adj. vs. not enough + noun. For example, they might compare "He isn't patient enough to endure the wait/waiting longer" vs. "He doesn't have enough patience to wait longer."

Passive voice

With upper intermediate and advanced classes, this picture context lends itself well to exercises using passive voice forms, as in the duplicatable worksheet on the back of *Picture 4*. Or develop something similar to fit the needs and level of your class.

Answer Key

2. Sam's new tennis racket was broken after only seven hours of play.
3. Fred's purchase has to be returned before the end of the month.
4. Lim's clock has to be repaired while it's still under warranty.
5. Carla's shoes will be exchanged because they're too big.
6. Mrs. Lee's new toaster has to be fixed because the cord was damaged before she bought it.

Note: See *Additional Language Development Exercises*, pp. 95–97, for pronunciation practice to accompany this picture.

---

5 Getting on the Bus

Differences

(Circled in *bottom* picture, left to right)

1. woman shorter   2. no hat   3. arm lower
4. bow instead of ruffles   5. skirt instead of pants
6. bag instead of book   7. "EXPRESS" instead of
"LOCAL"   8. more books

STUDENTS SHOULD DESCRIBE CHANGES IN
BOTTOM PICTURE. See pp. 1–3 for suggestions on
implementation in beginning, intermediate, and advanced classes.

Context Questions

Let students participate with you in creating a story
from this picture. Many of the questions below are
open-ended—there is no one right answer—in order
to encourage student involvement. Some questions
depend on interpretation of clues within the picture,
to encourage active thinking and attention to detail.

All questions are intended as guides only. You may
think of other ways of phrasing them for your students. Or you may think of other questions.

Class discussion resulting from such questions will
give you a chance to informally assess actual student
performance in various language skills and lifeskills,
with an eye to developing appropriate follow-up materials for the picture. (See pp. 3–4 for more details.)

FOLD PAPERS TO LOOK AT THE *TOP* PICTURE
ONLY.

- What time is it? Is it a weekday or a weekend?
  Why do you think so? (Presence of people
  dressed for work and students with books
  suggests a weekday, early morning or afternoon.)
- Where are the people going? What do they do?
  Why do you think so? (People going to work
  might include: construction worker or other laborer; nurse, dental assistant, or food-service
  worker; business or professional people [the
  woman in the suit could be a manager or a clerk].
  Others could be retired people, a bus company
  employee or policeman, and students.)
- What is the young man who is holding a map
  doing? (Asking directions.) Why do you think
  so?
- Where do you think the young man is going?
  (You might suggest that he is going for a job interview.) What kind of job, do you think? Why do
  you think so? What suggestions could you give
  him for a successful job interview?

Language Functions

Language functions describe what people *do* with the
language when they interact with each other.

Through structured dialogs, dialog development activities, and creative role play, we can give our students practice using the language in these different
ways in situations that are important for their lives.
Check the Table of Activities and Exercises for Language Development (following the Table of Contents),
for dialog activities found in this book.

Some functions appropriate to this picture are listed
below. You may think of others. The examples given
for each function are intended to stimulate your thinking. Reword them as necessary to fit your region of the
country, the abilities of your students, and your particular lesson. (See pp. 4–5 for more details.)

Asking directions: "Excuse/pardon me, where is/
can you tell me where...?"

Giving directions: "Go to the stop across the
street and take... Make a right at the next corner and
go down two blocks. It's right by the..."

Asking for change or the time: "Excuse me, do
you have the time/know what time it is?...Do you
have change for a dollar?" (*Note*: Depending on where

5
Getting on the Bus

Can you find EIGHT differences between these pictures?

Understanding Pronouns and Making *Yes/No* Questions

Directions:
1. Read the sentences to yourself.
2. Ask your teacher or your friends about words you don't know.
3. Read the sentences aloud. Tell what the pronouns are and what they mean.
4. Make Yes/No questions from the sentences.
5. Read your questions aloud.

1. Some of these people are waiting in line.
2. They're going to work.
3. A couple of them are retired.
4. An older man is getting off the bus.
5. An older woman is waiting for him.
6. She is talking to a little girl.
7. The little girl is her granddaughter.

8. Many of these people take the bus five days a week.
9. Some of them go to school.
10. One man has a job interview downtown today.
11. He wants to know how to get there by bus.
12. The policeman knows how.

13. He will tell him where to go.
14. Everyone will be on time for work and school today.
15. It will be a good day for everyone.

16. Yesterday was a bad time for everyone here.
17. The buses were late then.

18. People waited for them for a long time.
19. The policeman asked a lot of people to wait some more.
20. Some of them told him where to go.

you teach, it may be appropriate to distinguish between change for a certain amount, and the spare-change request of a panhandler.)

Responding politely to an easy request: "Yes, it's 8:20...Well, let me see...Yes, I have it. Here...No, I'm sorry, I can't help you..."

Complaining: "I'm so tired of waiting...I wish these people would hurry up...This bus is always late...I've got to get to _____ and start _____." (This might be an internal monologue—a character's thoughts—rather than an external dialog.)

Making small talk: "Nice day, isn't it?...Did you see _____ on TV last night?...Did you hear/read about _____ in the news this morning?...Think we'll make it to work/school on time? The last two buses went right on by..."

Lifeskills Extensions

See *Appendix 3*, pp. 104–08, for a list of specific lifeskills competencies and published materials that suggest activities appropriate for this context.

Comparing transportation systems: Discuss the public transportation system in your area. If more than one exists, have students compare them for price, speed, and convenience.

Story problems using maps and schedules: Collect public transportation route maps and time/fare schedules, if available, and use them for problem-solving activities.

Example
I live near _____ and I want to go to _____ . I need to be there at _____ A.M./P.M. What time should I start? Will I need to transfer? How much money will I need?

Listening comprehension: Many metropolitan transportation systems have phone services where passengers may call for information on bus routes, times, and fares. If such a service exists in your area, make several calls, noting the wording and speed of the speaker's speech. Then, reconstruct the dialog on tape with a partner. Try not to sound like an ESL teacher!

Further Language Development

Pattern drills

Make up statements about *Picture 5: Getting on the Bus*, or copy statements from the duplicatable exercise on

the back of *Picture 5*, and write them on the board. Ask your high-beginning and intermediate students to:
- repeat each statement, adding a time word;
- change singular to plural/plural to singular/"he" to "she" (or insert possessive or object pronouns, if students have studied them);
- make each statement negative or a question (or, if a statement is negative or a question, ask students to make it affirmative).

All the above drills can be repeated, contrasting the simple present tense with the present, past, and/or future tenses.

Understanding pronouns and making *Yes/No* questions

Use the duplicatable exercise on the back of *Picture 5* and follow these steps with your high-beginning or intermediate students:
1. Read the sentences for general meaning, vocabulary discussion, pronunciation, and intonation.
2. Identify and discuss the pronouns and what they refer to.
3. With student participation, make the sentences into *Yes/No* questions.
   Example
   - Are some of these people waiting in line? (**Yes**)
   - Is everyone going to work? (**No**)
   - Do you see three retired people? (**No**)

     Note that each section of sentences, separated by a line, requires somewhat different manipulations because of differences in verbs and tenses. This exercise as presented is more appropriate for review, pulling together work done earlier in separate sessions, than as an exercise to learn *Yes/No* question formation for the first time. It can be simplified for more beginning groups by using fewer tenses and focusing either on "BE" verbs and those that take BE as their auxiliary in the present or past, or focusing on verbs that take DO in its present or past form as their auxiliary.
4. Write the questions on the board, asking students to read them aloud to practice the rising intonation of *Yes/No* questions.

Note: See *Additional Language Development Exercises*, pp. 95–97, for simple present tense and frequency adverb practice to accompany this picture.

---

6 Riding on the Bus

Differences

(Circled in *bottom* picture, left to right)

1. arm lower   **2.** no faces in ad   **3.** young man heavier   **4.** cart handle longer   **5.** no umbrella
6. sign different   **7.** no head phones, or headset
8. bald man looking to left

STUDENTS SHOULD DESCRIBE CHANGES IN *BOTTOM* PICTURE. See pp. 1–3 for suggestions on implementation in beginning, intermediate, and advanced classes.

Context Questions

Let students participate with you in creating a story from this picture. Many of the questions below are open-ended—there is no one right answer— in order to encourage student involvement. Some questions depend on interpretation of clues within the picture, to encourage active thinking and attention to detail.

All questions are intended as guides only. You may think of other ways of phrasing them for your students. Or you may think of other questions.

Class discussion resulting from such questions will give you a chance to informally assess actual student performance in various language skills and lifeskills, with an eye to developing appropriate follow-up materials for the picture. (See pp. 3–4 for more details.)

FOLD PAPERS TO LOOK AT THE *TOP* PICTURE ONLY.
- Where are these people? Why do you think so?
- What time could it be? Do you think it could be early in the morning? Why or why not? (Presence of passengers with groceries would suggest that it is somewhat later in the day.)
- What is the man with the mustache holding in his hand? (It could be a bus pass or transfer, but it is more likely to be a one-dollar bill, or a five or a ten, as the bus driver is frowning and pointing to the "Exact Fare Only" sign.)

Teacher-guided student questions

Try having students themselves ask questions of each other while you listen and help as needed. Put students in pairs and give each a different list of questions to alternately ask a partner, as in this example for low–intermediate classes. One student is **A**, the other is **B**. **A** reads a question on her/his list; **B** looks at the picture and responds. Then **B** asks a question from her/his list; **A** looks at the picture and responds.

Example*

A. ASK YOUR PARTNER THESE QUESTIONS, BUT DON'T SHOW YOUR PAPER TO HER/HIM.
- How many people are driving the bus?
- Which person is wearing a cap?
- Who looks tired? Why?
- Which person is carrying groceries?
- How many people are wearing glasses? Where are they?
- Which person has a mustache? What does he want to do?
- Who is saying, "Excuse me"?

B. ASK YOUR PARTNER THESE QUESTIONS, BUT DON'T SHOW YOUR PAPER TO HER/HIM.
- How many passengers are there on the bus?
- Who has a radio?
- Is the bus driver happy? Why?

---

*Thanks to the anonymous colleague who passed this exercise to me on the stairs one day between classes.

6
Riding on the Bus

Can you find EIGHT differences between these pictures?

Writing Sentences with Adjectives

Read the two sentences after each number below. Write them together to make one sentence. The first two are done for you.

1. The man is young. The man is carrying bags.
   The young man is carrying bags.

2. The bus is old. Many people are riding on the bus.
   Many people are riding on the old bus.

3. The young man is unhappy. The young man bumped the guy next to him.
   _____

4. That guy is big. That guy is getting angry.
   _____

5. The woman is old. The woman has to stand up.
   _____

6. The old woman is tired. Nobody gave a seat to the old woman.
   _____

7. One passenger is new. That passenger doesn't have change.
   _____

8. One passenger is new. Do you have change for the passenger?
   _____

Can you put all of the following sentences together to make one sentence? Try.

The man is unhappy. The man is young. The man bumped a guy on the bus. The guy is big. The guy is angry. The bus is old.

_____

_____

_____

Now draw a line under the adjectives in all the sentences you wrote.

_____

- Which person has groceries in a cart?
- How many people are standing up? Why?
- Which person is smoking? Should s/he smoke?
- How many people look angry? Where are they?
- Why do they look angry?
- Who is saying, "Hey, be careful!"

Language Functions

Language functions describe what people *do* with the language when they interact with each other.

Through structured dialogs, dialog development activities, and creative role play, we can give our students practice using the language in these different ways in situations that are important for their lives. Check the Table of Activities and Exercises for Language Development (following the Table of Contents), for dialog activities found in this book.

Some functions appropriate to this picture are listed below. You may think of others. The examples given for each function are intended to stimulate your thinking. Reword them as necessary to fit your region of the country, the abilities of your students, and your particular lesson. (See pp. 4–5 for more details.)

Expressing displeased surprise: "Hey!...Watch out!...Look out!...Watch it!"

Apologizing: "Oops, sorry!...Oh, excuse me! ...Sorry, got my hands full here..."

Asking for clarification: "Is this the bus to _____ ?... How much is the fare?...Can you give me change?"

Giving clarification: "Yes, this is the one/No, you want bus number _____ ...Sorry, I can't give change...Look, mister, read the sign!"

Offering: (What somebody *should* say) "Would you like this seat?...Here, ma'am, sit down..."

Lifeskills Extensions

See *Appendix 3*, pp. 104–08, for a list of specific lifeskills competencies and published materials that suggest activities appropriate for this context.

Bring in tokens, transfers, and bus passes for discussion.

Story problems using math: Develop lifeskills math problems appropriate to your students' level and the area in which they live.

Example

Miguel works three days a week in _____ _____ . He sometimes visits his in-laws on weekends in _____ . These are the only times he takes the bus. He lives in _____ .

Is it cheaper for Miguel to buy a monthly pass or to pay the fare each time he goes?

Further Language Development

Adjective placement before nouns

For beginning classes, the placement of adjectives before nouns can be difficult. Try the duplicatable worksheet on the back of *Picture 6*, or develop something similar. Student sentences will vary.

-ed vs. -ing adjectives

For intermediate and advanced students, the distinction between adjectives ending in -ed and those ending in -ing is confusing. The content of *Picture 6* lends itself to explanations of this difference and practice of statements such as:

Example
1. The big guy is irritated. It's irritating to be bumped.
2. The young man with the bags is embarrassed. It's embarrassing to bump into people on the bus.

After explanation of this grammar, you could proceed with an exercise that includes examples 1–5, but in this form:
3. The older woman is tired. It's _____ to stand up on the bus after shopping.
4. The bus driver is _____ . It's annoying to repeat the same thing all day.
5. The new passenger is confused. It's _____ to learn a new bus system.

Modal auxiliaries (*can, should, might, and the like*)

For review with intermediate and advanced classes, list modals on the board and have students use them to make their own sentences about *Picture 6*. Or make an exercise like this:

Example
1. People (can't) get change from the bus driver.
2. They (must/have to) have the exact fare.
3. Somebody (should) give a seat to that woman.
4. She (must/could/might) be worn out from shopping.
5. Somebody (might/may) get off soon and then she (might/may) get a seat.
6. People (shouldn't) smoke or play their radios on the bus, but sometimes they do.

7 A Supermarket Aisle

Differences

(Circled in *bottom* picture, left to right)

1. no boxes   **2.** no sign   **3.** fewer children   **4.** tee shirt has sleeves   **5.** coffee more expensive*   **6.** tie stripes going other way   **7.** fruit weighs more (or scales different)   **8.** carrots less expensive*

STUDENTS SHOULD DESCRIBE CHANGES IN *BOTTOM* PICTURE. See pp. 1–3 for suggestions on implementation in beginning, intermediate, and advanced classes.

Context Questions

Let students participate with you in creating a story from this picture. Many of the questions below are open-ended—there is no one right answer—in order to encourage student involvement. Some questions depend on interpretation of clues within the picture, to encourage active thinking and attention to detail.

These differences can be used to introduce a lesson on unit prices. (See exercise on p. 33.)

All questions are intended as guides only. You may think of other ways of phrasing them for your students. Or you may think of other questions.

Class discussion resulting from such questions will give you a chance to informally assess actual student performance in various language skills and lifeskills, with an eye to developing appropriate follow-up materials for the picture. (See pp. 3–4 for more details.)

FOLD PAPERS TO LOOK AT THE *TOP* PICTURE ONLY.

- Where are these people? Why do you think so?
- What time of day is it? Why do you think so?
- What are the two men doing?
- What are the children doing?
- What is the woman doing? What is her relationship to the children? Look at her face. How do you think she feels?
- What does the man in the suit want to do? How do you think he feels? Why do you think so?

Language Functions

Language functions describe what people *do* with the language when they interact with each other.

Through structured dialogs, dialog development activities, and creative role play, we can give our students practice using the language in these different ways in situations that are important for their lives. Check the Table of Activities and Exercises for Language Development (following the Table of Contents), for dialog activities found in this book.

Some functions appropriate to this picture are listed below. You may think of others. The examples given for each function are intended to stimulate your thinking. Reword them as necessary to fit your region of the country, the abilities of your students, and your particular lesson. (See pp. 4–5 for more details.)

Politely asking strangers for reasonable action: "Excuse me, can you let me through?...Pardon me, I need to get by...Say, folks, I'm in a hurry..." (*Note*: In native-speaker interaction, the first request would most likely be "Excuse me," since what is wanted is obvious. Only if the speaker is ignored the first time is the request likely to be made more explicit.)

Asking a friend for an opinion or preference: "What do you think of this, Bruce? We had it last week at Randy's."

Expressing mild disagreement or disapproval: "Well, I think something drier would be better with dinner tonight."

Expressing strong disagreement or disapproval: "That stuff? Never!"

Reprimanding children: "Keep it down, kids. I've got a headache...Mikey, quit teasing your sister

7
A Supermarket Aisle

Can you find EIGHT differences between these pictures?

Compare the Supermarket Specials This Week

	DUCKY MARKET		SAFE-BET STORE		PAYWAY SUPER	
COFFEE	Bilger's 1 lb. can	$3.49	Mountain Sisters 2 lbs	$4.89	Webonne 2 lbs	$5.19
RICE	Honide 5 lb. bag	$2.19	Willard's Pick 1 lb. box	$ .69	Pam's Best 1 lb	$ .89
LETTUCE	1 head iceberg	$ .79	2 heads Boston redleaf	$ .99	1 head Romaine	$ .75
GROUND BEEF	1 lb	$1.89	5 lb. package	$7.99	2 lbs.	$3.05
COOKING OIL	Lestor Brand 1 qt.	$ .93	Snafu Brand 1 qt.	$ .67	Wezin Oil 1 gal.	$3.59
BABY FOOD	Matthew's Own 5 jars	$1.30	Aurora Brand 8 jars	$2.00	Molly's Munch 1 jar	$ .29

Fill in the blanks below. Use phrases like *cheaper than* and *the cheapest; more expensive than* and *the most expensive.* Find the answers in the advertisement above. The first two have been done for you.

1. The coffee at Safe-Bet Store is _cheaper than the coffee at_ Payway Super.

2. The coffee at Ducky Market is _the most expensive_ .

3. The rice at Ducky Market is _____ .

4. The lettuce at Safe-Bet Store is _____ Payway Super and _____ .

5. The ground beef at Ducky Market is _____ .

6. The oil at Safe-Bet Store is _____ .

7. The baby food at Ducky Market is _____ Safe-Bet Store.

Now make three sentences of your own. Use the advertisement above.

8. _____ .

9. _____ .

10. _____ .

... Sherry, stop whining. Do you want to wait in the car?"

Lifeskills Extensions

See *Appendix 3*, pp. 104–08, for specific lifeskills competencies and published materials that suggest activities appropriate for this picture context.

Price checking: Make a list of ten to twenty items that your students are likely to buy. Check prices at a nearby supermarket and add them to your list.

Give students a worksheet listing the items without prices. Read your list of items with prices to the class, at native-speaker speed, instructing students to write down the prices next to the items as they hear them. Repeat if necessary, but don't slow down your speech.

For follow-up, repeat the exercise a week or two later, with students using the same worksheets. Check the prices again before doing the exercise, and read the new prices that you found. Have students note which items went up or down in price, and which stayed the same.

Comparison shopping: With your class, list several nearby supermarkets where your students are likely to shop. Then make a list of five to ten items that your students are likely to buy. Get the prices of these items at each supermarket by checking the ads, going to the markets yourself to get prices, and/or assigning students to check on prices and report them the next day. Use this information for an exercise to practice cheaper/cheapest and more/most expensive.

Variation 1: Use the duplicatable Supermarket Specials worksheet* on the back of *Picture 7*, or develop something similar that fits the needs and level of your class.

Answer Key
3. the cheapest.
4. cheaper than the lettuce at/Ducky Market.
5. the most expensive.
6. the cheapest.
7. more expensive than the baby food at

Variation 2: Figure unit pricing of local supermarket items, starting with the examples in the picture: "Which is a better buy—a pound of coffee at $3.69 or 16 oz. at $4.69?" "3 lbs. of carrots for 98¢, or 2 lbs. for 63¢?" "A 48-oz. bottle of oil for $3.99, or a 24-oz. bottle on special for $1.29?" and the like.

Special thanks to Roger E. Winn-Bell Olsen, who helped with prices, brand names, and general morale.

Picture 7: A Supermarket Aisle

Further Language Development

Listening comprehension (Picture grids)

Two students, or two teams, each have a set of small pictures identical to those of the other(s). They also each have a grid of squares, marked off on large manila folders, on which to put the pictures. (See the illustration.) There is a barrier between the two grids so that **A** cannot see **B**'s grid. (The cover flap of a manila folder makes a handy barrier.)

A arranges its pictures on its grid, then tells **B** where to put its identical pictures so that the arrangement will be the same. In lower-level classes, you may want to allow **A** to watch **B** as it follows **A**'s directions so that **A** can make directions clearer if necessary. In a really challenging activity, neither side is allowed to see the other's grid until all instructions have been given and followed. Then the two teams compare their arrangements.

The difficulty of the game also depends on the complexity of the grid. Beginners should start with a nine-square grid, and be taught the terms <u>top</u>, <u>center</u>, <u>bottom</u>, <u>left</u>, and <u>right</u>, with some practice in saying "top, left, center, right," and "top left, top right," and the like. More advanced students can work with twenty-square or twenty-four-square grids and use the terms <u>above</u>, <u>column</u>, <u>row</u>, <u>square</u>, <u>over</u>, <u>under</u>, <u>between</u>, <u>first</u>, <u>second</u>, <u>third</u>, and the like.

The content of the pictures also influences the degree of difficulty. Pictures that are distinctly different from each other are easier to identify than are pictures that have similar elements.

More complete instructions on designing grid sets with manila folders are given in *Communication-Starters* (Olsen, 1977).

A Supermarket Checkout Counter

Differences

(Circled in *bottom* picture, left to right)

1. carton of ice cream or cottage cheese instead of milk
2. man slimmer or thinner   3. sign different
4. no eggs   5. belt different   6. no jam
7. bagger's head turned other way   8. more groceries in bag

STUDENTS SHOULD DESCRIBE CHANGES IN *BOTTOM* PICTURE. See pp. 1–3 for suggestions on implementation in beginning, intermediate, and advanced classes.

Context Questions

Let students participate with you in creating a story from this picture. Many of the questions below are open-ended—there is no one right answer—in order to encourage student involvement. Some questions depend on interpretation of clues within the picture, to encourage active thinking and attention to detail.

All questions are intended as guides only. You may think of other ways of phrasing them for your students. Or you may think of other questions.

Class discussion resulting from such questions will give you a chance to informally assess actual student performance in various language skills and lifeskills, with an eye to developing appropriate follow-up materials for the picture. (See pp. 3–4 for more details.)

FOLD PAPERS TO LOOK AT THE *TOP* PICTURE ONLY.

- Where are these people? Why do you think so?
- What are they doing? (Describe each person's actions.)
- Is something wrong? What do you think it is?
- What do you think the people should do about it?
- Has that ever happened to you? What did you do?

Language Functions

Language functions describe what people *do* with the language when they interact with each other.

Through structured dialogs, dialog development activities, and creative role play, we can give our students practice using the language in these different ways in situations that are important for their lives. Check the Table of Activities and Exercises for Language Development (following the Table of Contents), for dialog activities found in this book.

Some functions appropriate to this picture are listed below. You may think of others. The examples given for each function are intended to stimulate your thinking. Reword them as necessary to fit your region of the country, the abilities of your students, and your particular lesson. (See pp. 4–5 for more details.)

Politely requesting an easy favor: "Excuse me, do you mind if I go ahead of you? I've just got one item...Could I cut in front of you? I'm in sort of a hurry..."

Complying with an easy request: "Sure, go ahead...Yes, that's all right...Be my guest..."

Expressing dismay: "Oh no! Where's my checkbook?...Oh dear, I was *sure* I had enough money with me...Oh-oh, I think my wallet's been stolen..."

Expressing annoyance indirectly: "Look, lady, what do you want me to do?...C'mon, there are a lot of people behind you..."

Expressing helpful concern: "Can't find your money, ma'am? Take your time...We can hold this for you if you want to come back...Let me call the manager."

Lifeskills Extensions

See *Appendix 3*, pp. 104–08, for a list of specific lifeskills competencies and published materials that suggest activities appropriate for this picture context.

8
A Supermarket Checkout Counter

Can you find EIGHT differences between these pictures?

Applying for a Supermarket Check-Cashing Card

Betty Garcia wants to get a check-cashing card at the Ducky Market. She wants to cash personal checks and payroll checks there.

Betty's husband's name is Rick. They live at 2439 Elmore Avenue in Oakland, California 94611. Their home phone is 611-0980.

Betty works at Oakwood Shoe Distributors at 180 Piedmont Avenue in Oakland. Her husband works across the street at Purple Printers, 177 Piedmont Avenue. Betty's phone number at work is 432-9981 and Rick's is 432-6180.

Betty doesn't drive, but Rick does. His driver's license number is A3344189. Betty just got her Social Security card two months ago, when she started working. Her number is 576-91-7433.

Betty and Rick have a MasterCard, number 2281-0334-8039-7876, but they don't have a VISA card yet. They also have a charge account at Sears Roebuck, card number 27-98542-12457-2.

They also have an account at the National Functional Bank, at 899 Wilkins Drive, Oakland 94612.

Help Betty fill out her application form below.

DUCKY MARKET Check-Cashing Card
APPLICATION

PRINT LAST NAME	YOUR FIRST NAME	SPOUSE'S FIRST NAME IF APPLICABLE	HOME PHONE

YOUR SIGNATURE | SPOUSE'S SIGNATURE | YOUR WORK PHONE

ADDRESS | CITY | ZIP | SPOUSE WORK PHONE

YOUR EMPLOYER _____ BANK _____

ADDRESS _____

SPOUSE'S EMPLOYER _____ ADDRESS _____

ADDRESS _____

MASTERCARD NO. _____ CITY _____ STATE _____ ZIP _____

VISA NO. _____

CREDIT CARD _____

_____

YOUR DR. LIC. NO. _____ ACCT. NO. _____

LOW ☐ MEDIUM ☐ HIGH ☐ No. Returned Checks ____

SPOUSE'S DR. LIC. NO. _____ TWO FIGURES ☐ THREE FIGURES ☐ FOUR FIGURES ☐

FIVE FIGURES ☐

SOC. SEC. NO. _____ DATE ACCT. OPENED _____

BANK CERTIFICATION STAMP HERE ↓

Card remains property of Ducky Market

Categorizing meat and poultry

Upper-beginning and intermediate students are often confused by the many terms for different kinds of meat. Often an ad will not use the words "beef," "pork," "chicken," or "turkey" at all. Check the ads and supermarket signs to see what terms are used in your area. Then try an exercise like this:

Example

Here are some names for meat at the supermarket. Write B for beef, P for pork, or C for chicken or turkey.

____ 1. T-bone, tender and juicy
____ 2. self-basting tender toms
____ 3. standing rib roast
____ 4. cut-up fryers, 5-lb. bag
____ 5. honey-smoked butts
____ 6. best Canadian bacon
____ 7. sirloin tips
____ 8. extra lean chops
____ 9. Cornish game hens
____10. New York strip

Reading for information/filling out forms

Use the duplicatable application for a check-cashing card exercise on the back of *Picture 8* to give your upper-beginning and intermediate students practice in an important lifeskill. Or develop something similar that fits the needs and level of your class.

Categorizing cleaning products by their use

Here is a hands-on activity for use with beginning, intermediate, and advanced students. Bring in a variety of cleaning products for household or personal use, including different brands of the same product. Put a letter on each container for identification. First make a master letter/product "key" for yourself; then put the containers in different parts of the room.

Make a list (to be duplicated) of statements such as:
1. It's for washing windows._____
2. It's for washing your hair. _____
3. It's for cleaning toilets. _____
4. It's for brushing your teeth. _____
5. It's for waxing floors. _____

Give students copies of the list and go over all the statements with them, making sure that they understand the words and where to write the letters of the products that the words describe. (In lower-level classes, use products and pantomime to explain.) Provide ample time for students to inspect the product containers and to try categorizing them on their lists. By putting containers in different parts of the room, you spread students out and give them a better chance to inspect everything closely.

In lower-level classes, it is more important for students to be able to identify products by their use (this involves a finite group of statements with relatively simple vocabulary) than by their product name or generic name (which involves a list that is much longer, and harder to pronounce and remember). Use the patterns "Is this for _____ -ing?" and "Can I _____ with this?" to help beginners acquire information on household products.

Recycle this activity frequently by adding new containers and deleting ones that are familiar to all. Students will often question you about other products they need. (One father recently asked how to get his children's crayon marks off the walls.) Animated native-language interaction may be motivated by this kind of activity. If it occurs, let students continue uninterrupted for awhile; then ask them to summarize their conversations for you *in English*.

Further Language Development

Quantifiers

The top version of *Picture 8* is especially rich in words that take quantifiers of measure: a <u>dozen</u> eggs, a <u>jar</u> of jam, <u>rolls</u> of toilet paper, and so on. Use it to introduce or practice quantifiers.

Example

A: Do you see any toothpaste?
B: Yes, I see a <u>tube</u> of toothpaste.
A: Do you see any tomatoes?
B: Yes, I see a <u>can</u> of tomatoes and a <u>basket</u> of cherry tomatoes.

In more advanced classes, go over the picture for review, then ask students to recall the items and their quantifiers without looking at their papers. This is a stimulating small-group activity, especially as a contest: Give a prize to the student or team that can recall and write down the most items in three minutes. Inexpensive candies, balloons, or novelties make appropriate prizes.

Note: See *Additional Language Development Exercises*, pp. 95–97, for practice in dialog development through paraphrase to accompany this picture.

Picture 8: A Supermarket Checkout Counter

A Clinic Waiting Room

Differences

(Circled in *bottom* picture, left to right)

1. less hair or balder   2. sandals instead of shoes
3. legs crossed the other way   4. bandage on the
other eye   5. little girl's hair shorter   6. more
papers   7. no glasses   8. no watch

STUDENTS SHOULD DESCRIBE CHANGES IN
BOTTOM PICTURE. See pp. 1–3 for suggestions on
implementation in beginning, intermediate, and advanced classes.

Context Questions

Let students participate with you in creating a story
from this picture. Many of the questions below are
open-ended—there is no one right answer—in order
to encourage student involvement. Some questions
depend on interpretation of clues within the picture,
to encourage active thinking and attention to detail.

All questions are intended as guides only. You may
think of other ways of phrasing them for your students. Or you may think of other questions.

Class discussion resulting from such questions will
give you a chance to informally assess actual student
performance in various language skills and lifeskills,
with an eye to developing appropriate follow-up materials for the picture. (See pp. 3–4 for more details.)

FOLD PAPERS TO LOOK AT THE *TOP* PICTURE
ONLY.

- Where are these people? Why do you think so?
- Who is the woman with the telephone? Why do
  you think so? Whom could she be talking to?
- Who is the woman signing the paper? What kind
  of paper could she be signing?
- Who are the people on the couch? Why are they
  sitting down? Are they sick?
- What is the man doing to the little girl?

Note: See suggestions in *Further Language Development*,
p. 41, for an alternative way to introduce the picture.

Language Functions

Language functions describe what people *do* with the
language when they interact with each other.

Through structured dialogs, dialog development activities, and creative role play, we can give our students practice using the language in these different
ways in situations that are important for their lives.
Check the Table of Activities and Exercises for Language Development (following the Table of Contents),
for dialog activities found in this book.

Some functions appropriate to this picture are listed
below. You may think of others. The examples given
for each function are intended to stimulate your thinking. Reword them as necessary to fit your region of the
country, the abilities of your students, and your particular lesson. (See pp. 4–5 for more details.)

Answering a business call/giving information:
"Hello, City Clinic... Yes, we're open until 6 P.M.
today... Yes, we have a twenty-four-hour emergency
room... No, you don't need an appointment..."

Asking for health information on the telephone:
"How long have you had the pain?... Have you come
in to see us before?... Who is your regular doctor?... Can you get down here this afternoon?..."

Reassuring and encouraging: "My, you're getting
to be a big girl!... You've grown two inches this
year!..."

Asking for clarification of procedure: "Where do I
sign?... Will my insurance cover this?... Will he be all
right?... How long should he keep the bandage
on?... When should we come back?..."

Requesting more specific information: "We need
your Social Security number, ma'am... Is this your
current address?... You need to sign here at the
bottom..."

Look Again Pictures

9
A Clinic Waiting Room

Can you find EIGHT differences between these pictures?

Vocabulary-Picture Matching

Match the statements below with what they identify in the picture.
Find the number or numbers in the picture that go with each statement.
Write the numbers on the line next to each statement.

(Note: Some statements may be matched with more than one person,
and a person may be matched with more than one statement.)

____ a. They are injured.

____ b. She is pregnant.

____ c. They are busy.

____ d. They are at work.

____ e. She is filling out forms.

____ f. She is being measured.

____ g. She is answering the phone.

____ h. It means "no smoking."

____ i. This person has striped pants.

____ j. This person has plaid pants.

____ k. This person has a paisley print dress.

____ l. This person has an argyle sweater.

Lifeskills Extensions

See *Appendix 3*, pp. 104–08, for a list of specific lifeskills competencies and published materials that suggest activities appropriate for this picture context.

Listing local clinics and emergency hospitals

Make a list of clinics and emergency hospitals in your area, including addresses and appropriate phone numbers. Give a list to each student. Together, practice pronunciation of the names. Have a city map available for student use. Ask information questions, such as, "Hung, what's the number of St. Mary's Clinic?" "Lee, where is City Emergency?" "Juan, which hospital is closest to your house?"

Or post a city map on the wall. If possible, make copies for students, and also make an overhead transparency. Find the clinics and hospitals on the map. Have students tell you the locations: "It's on _____ between _____ and _____." Have students tell you how to get to a particular clinic or hospital location from their house: "Go down _____, turn right, go for twenty blocks and _____..."

Roleplaying emergency calls

Make a list of roleplay situations. Have students roleplay calls to clinics and private doctors, with you taking the part of the telephone receptionist. Since it will be challenging for different students to roleplay the same part, your list need not be endless. Students often have suggestions for situations that they would like to practice roleplaying. Here are some possibilities:

Example
1. Call St. Mercy Medical Clinic to find out what days and hours it is open.
2. You feel dizzy and tired and you have had a fever of 102°F (or 39°C) for nearly a day. Call the clinic and ask what to do.
3. Your baby is supposed to have a well-baby checkup tomorrow, but you can't come in then. Call and change the appointment.
4. Your husband/wife pulled a muscle in his/her back this morning and can barely walk. Call the clinic and ask what to do.

As you roleplay the telephone receptionist, you will probably find yourself asking a lot of questions that begin, "When did you..." or "How long have you...?" You can use these forms as the basis for student practice with the past tense ("When did you fall?") and the present perfect ("How long have you had a fever?").

In an intermediate/advanced roleplay situation, you might reverse your role and become the caller while your stronger students play the part of the telephone receptionist (modeling themselves after the strong role you presented in earlier role plays).

Further Language Development

Vocabulary—picture matching

This particular matching exercise is actually a variation on introducing a picture, but it can also be used for further language practice.

Using the top version of *Picture 9*, make a matching exercise like this:

Example 1
DRAW A LINE FROM THESE WORDS TO THE PART OF THE PICTURE THAT THEY IDENTIFY:

1. sling **2.** crutch **3.** bandage **4.** sign **5.** scales

6. desk **7.** couch **8.** papers **9.** phone

10. uniform **11.** maternity top

Use the duplicatable student worksheet on the back of *Picture 9* for an additional matching exercise, or develop something similar that fits the needs and level of your class.

Answer Key
a. 1, 4 **b.** 2 **c.** 5, 7, 8 **d.** 7, 8 **e.** 5 **f.** 6 **g.** 8
h. 3 **i.** 6 **j.** 2 **k.** 5 **l.** 4

10 Talking to the Doctor

Class discussion resulting from such questions will give you a chance to informally assess actual student performance in various language skills and lifeskills, with an eye to developing appropriate follow-up materials for the picture. (See pp. 3–4 for more details.)

FOLD PAPERS TO LOOK AT THE *TOP* PICTURE ONLY.

- Where are these people? Why do you think so?
- Why are they there? Why do you think so?
- Who is the woman in the glasses? What is she doing? Why is she doing that?
- Who is the man with his hands in his pocket? What is he doing? Why is he doing that?
- Who is the woman standing by the table? What is she doing? Why is she doing that?
- What's the matter with the little boy? (Be as specific as you can.) Why do you think so?

Language Functions

Language functions describe what people *do* with the language when they interact with each other.

Through structured dialogs, dialog development activities, and creative role play, we can give our students practice using the language in these different ways in situations that are important for their lives. Check the Table of Activities and Exercises for Language Development (following the Table of Contents), for dialog activities found in this book.

Some functions appropriate to this picture are listed below. You may think of others. The examples given for each function are intended to stimulate your thinking. Reword them as necessary to fit your region of the country, the abilities of your students, and your particular lesson. (See pp. 4–5 for more details.)

Asking for information about someone's illness: "When did he get those spots, Mr. Ritti?... How long has he had a fever?... When did he start feeling dizzy?... Does anyone else in your family feel that way? ... Does he have any allergies?... Has he had shots for...?"

Describing symptoms of an illness: "We saw the spots on his chest this morning... His fever started last night... He said he felt dizzy this morning..."

Giving instructions: "Now I want you to give him a teaspoon of this four times a day... Rub this on his rash after he's had a hot bath... Give him two capsules in the morning and evening just after he eats... Follow the directions on the label..."

Asking for clarification: "How many times a day, doctor?... What's the name of this medicine?... Where can I get it?... Should he stay in bed?... Can other people get sick from him?... Wait, doctor, could you pronounce that one more time?..."

Differences

(Circled in *bottom* picture, left to right)

1. no window   **2.** no pockets   **3.** bottle instead of box   **4.** coat longer   **5.** no spots or rash   **6.** hand below knee   **7.** middle "E" pointed other way **8.** table legs shorter (*Note*: <u>boy's legs</u> vs. <u>table legs</u> or <u>legs of the table</u>)

STUDENTS SHOULD DESCRIBE CHANGES IN *BOTTOM* PICTURE. See pp. 1–3 for suggestions on implementation in beginning, intermediate, and advanced classes.

Context Questions

Let students participate with you in creating a story from this picture. Many of the questions below are open-ended—there is no one right answer—in order to encourage student involvement. Some questions depend on interpretation of clues within the picture, to encourage active thinking and attention to detail.

All questions are intended as guides only. You may think of other ways of phrasing them for your students. Or you may think of other questions.

10
Talking to the Doctor

Can you find EIGHT differences between these pictures?

Four-by-Four Dialogs

1.

    A.   Doctor, how is Billy?

    B.   He'll be fine in a week or so. Start him on this today.

    A.   How much do I give him?

    B.   Follow the directions exactly. Don't stop until he finishes <u>all</u> of it.

2.

    A.   How is my son doing, doctor?

    B.   After a few days of this medicine, he'll feel a lot better.

    A.   What do I do with it?

    B.   Read the label carefully and do what the directions say. Be sure he takes <u>all</u> of it.

3.

    A.   Well, doctor, what do you think?

    B.   Right now he feels terrible, but the worst is over. Start giving him this right away.

    A.   How should he use this?

    B.   Read the instructions on the label. Follow then until <u>all</u> the medicine is gone.

4.

    A.   How's my brother, doctor?

    B.   Don't worry. Just keep him quiet for a few days and give him this. He'll be okay.

    A.   How often should he take it?

    B.   The directions say "one teaspoon every four hours." And make him take <u>all</u> of it, even when he starts feeling better.

Complaining: "Mommy, I feel hot and cold. I want to go home...I don't feel good..."

Comforting: "That's okay, honey, we're going home soon...You'll feel better soon, dear..."

Lifeskills Extensions

See *Appendix 3*, pp. 104–08, for a list of specific lifeskills competencies and published materials that suggest activities appropriate for this picture context.

Understanding labels on medication

Collect all the medicine containers you have, both for prescription and nonprescription medicine, and look at the labels. What words are used to describe what the medication is for and how much to take? These words are important "head words" for students to look for. They are probably not the same on all containers. Notice how little information is actually given about the remedy itself. Use this point to emphasize to students the importance of listening closely to the doctor's instructions and asking questions about anything that is not clear.

Choose a prescription drug label that is as informative as any you can find, and make *exact* duplicated copies for your students. (The patient's name, address, and other personal information can, of course, be changed.) Include the address and phone number of the pharmacy, the doctor's name, the prescription number, refill information, and the like. Also prepare a transparency (see *Appendix 5*, p. 110) or a large drawing of the label on newsprint to use as a visual aid in class. Make the drawing as close to the original as you can. Ask students questions about the medication, such as:

- What is the medication for? (Some labels may not be specific.)
- When should you take it? How often?
- What doctor told you to take it?
- Where did you get it? Can you get a refill? (Some labels indicate that a prescription may not be refilled.)
- If you want to get more medication from the pharmacy, what must you do?
- How do you open the container?

In an intermediate or advanced class, this activity will probably not take long. In a beginning class, it may take more than one session.

Variation: Have students examine actual, empty prescription and nonprescription drug containers. Focus follow-up questions on their comprehension of the directions, their ability to distinguish the name of the medication from its brand name (when they differ), their understanding of what the product is for, and their understanding of the difference between prescription and nonprescription drugs. Emphasize the need to finish any prescribed medication *completely* if the doctor so orders, not just to stop taking it as soon as one feels better. (See the four-by-four dialogs under *Further Language Development*, below, for an exercise focusing on this point.)

Further Language Development

Vocabulary*

Have students look for names of items, and words related to individuals, actions, and conditions that begin with the letter "p" in *Picture 10*.

Examples

picture	patients
prescription	physician
panel (door)	putting
pane (glass)	(arm around child)
(*Note*: <u>pain</u>)	(hands in pockets)
pockets	(hand on stomach)
pants	pointing
poster	pain
(eye chart/sign)	(*Note*: <u>pane</u>)
plaid (shirt)	problem(s)
parents	poor health
person(s)	perspective
people	(depth of picture)

As students discover words, write them on the board and then have the class use them in varied sentences and dialogs.

Four-by-four dialogs**

Duplicate the dialog sheet on the back of *Picture 10*, and distribute to students. In the four dialogs, the first line of each will go with the second, third, and fourth lines of the others, for a total of sixteen combinations. Students can practice each dialog as is, then mix and match. (*Note:* When assigning dialog parts, **A** is generally easier. Assign **B** to the more able students in the class.)

---

*Thanks to Janet Thornburg and Joan Wolfgang for the vocabulary activity.
**Thanks to Clare Schurner and Jack Wigfield for the ideas that inspired the design of the four-by-four dialogs.

11 Outside an Apartment

Differences

(Circled in *bottom* picture, left to right)

1. frowning instead of smiling   2. flowers shorter
3. trees taller   4. no jacket or sweater
5. "unfurn." instead of "furn."   6. upstairs men
are farther apart   7. child crying instead of sleeping
8. no curtains

STUDENTS SHOULD DESCRIBE CHANGES IN *BOTTOM* PICTURE. See pp. 1–3 for suggestions on implementation in beginning, intermediate, and advanced classes.

Context Questions

Let students participate with you in creating a story from this picture. Many of the questions below are open-ended—there is no one right answer—in order to encourage student involvement. Some questions depend on interpretation of clues within the picture, to encourage active thinking and attention to detail.

All questions are intended as guides only. You may think of other ways of phrasing them for your students. Or you may think of other questions.

Class discussion resulting from such questions will give you a chance to informally assess actual student performance in various language skills and lifeskills, with an eye to developing appropriate follow-up materials for the picture. (See pp. 3–4 for more details.)

FOLD PAPERS TO LOOK AT THE *BOTTOM* PICTURE ONLY.
- Where are these people? Why do you think so?
- Why is the man looking at a newspaper?
- Who is the woman with the child in her arms? Why is she pointing to the sign?
- How many people are in the picture? Tell where each person is and what s/he is doing. (*Note: watch* TV vs. *wash* windows as a pronunciation contrast.)
- Do you think the manager takes good care of the place? Why or why not? (Note landscaping.)
- Is this a good place for people with children or pets? Why or why not?
- Would you like to live there? Why or why not?

Language Functions

Language functions describe what people *do* with the language when they interact with each other.

Through structured dialogs, dialog development activities, and creative role play, we can give our students practice using the language in these different ways in situations that are important for their lives. Check the Table of Activities and Exercises for Language Development (following the Table of Contents), for dialog activities found in this book.

Some functions appropriate to this picture are listed below. You may think of others. The examples given for each function are intended to stimulate your thinking. Reword them as necessary to fit your region of the country, the abilities of your students, and your particular lesson. (See pp. 4–5 for more details.)

If your students interpret the foreground figures as a family:

Expressing hope: "Sure they do; see that little girl in the window?...There's the sign...Let's take a look."

If these figures are interpreted as a prospective renter and the landlady with her child:

Asking for information: "Is this the place advertised in the paper?...How many bedrooms?...How much is the rent?/security deposit?/cleaning deposit?...Does that include garbage and utilities?..."

Giving information: "This is the place...We've got two studios in front and a one-bedroom in back...Go up and take a look...There's my husband talking to someone else now..."

11
Outside an Apartment

FURN. APTS.
FOR RENT

Can you find EIGHT differences between these pictures?

UNFURN. APTS.
FOR RENT

What/How-Questions for Clarification

Mr. Ramirez is looking for a place to live. He's talking to the manager of an apartment building, but her baby is crying so loudly that Mr. Ramirez can't hear everything she is saying. He has to keep asking her to repeat the information.

Help him ask his questions. Use question words like *who, what, where, when, why, how much, how many,* and *how long.*

1. MANAGER: We have a nice studio available now. The rent is WAAAAAAAAAH!
   MR. RAMIREZ: Could you repeat that? *How much is the rent?*
   _____

2. MANAGER: We'll have another one next week in our other building. It's at WAAAAAAAAAAH!
   MR. RAMIREZ: I couldn't hear you. _____
   _____

3. MANAGER: The other one has WAAAAAAAAAAH! bedrooms.
   MR. RAMIREZ: Excuse me, _____
   _____

4. MANAGER: I can't show it to you today, but it'll be ready on WAAAAAAAAAAH!
   MR. RAMIREZ: I'm sorry, _____
   _____

5. MANAGER: And actually, the rent on that one is a little cheaper because WAAAAAAAAAAH!
   MR. RAMIREZ: I didn't catch that. _____
   _____

6. MANAGER: However, we do require renters to sign a lease for at least WAAAAAAAAAAH!
   MR. RAMIREZ: I beg your pardon, _____
   _____

7. MANAGER: You should go upstairs and talk to WAAAAAAAAAAH!
   MR. RAMIREZ: _____
   _____

Lifeskills Extensions

See *Appendix 3*, pp. 104–08, for a list of specific lifeskills competencies and published materials that suggest activities appropriate for this picture context.

Understanding rental ads

Bring in rental ads from local newspapers and discuss the abbreviations (2 BR, AEK, plus utils, and the like). Create a matching exercise by putting the abbreviations in one column and explanations of those abbreviations in another column for students to match.

Story problems

Make up story problems using duplicated copies of the rental ads for each student.

Example

Sue Finn is looking for a one-bedroom apartment. She is willing to pay between _____ and _____ a month. She has a dog.

Which of these rental ads would probably interest her? What number should she call? When should she call? Does she have to pay a fee?

Further Language Development

Vocabulary and dialog development

Picture 11 lends itself well to discussion of building maintenance with high-beginning and intermediate students. Try the following sample dialog between yourself (**T**) and students (**S**):

T: Suppose you're the manager of an apartment building and I ask you for a job as your maintenance person. What kinds of things would I have to take care of?

S: Windows.

T: Okay, windows. What would I have to do?

S: Wash them.

T: Okay, "Wash the windows." (Write on board.) What would I use to wash them?

Some students might volunteer the word "water," but probably not "squeegee" and "pail." Add "with a squeegee and water in a pail" to the phrase on the board. Other sentences you could include are:

- Cut the grass with a lawn mower.
- Trim the shrubbery with hedge clippers.
- Water the plants with a hose.
- Sweep the walk with a broom.
- Clean the Venetian blinds with a sponge.
- Clean the carpets with rug shampoo, and so on.

Follow-up exercises for beginning classes might include Yes/No and Either/Or questions, such as: "Can I sweep the walk with hedge clippers?" "Do I clean the carpets with a lawn mower or with rug shampoo?" Advanced students could try to recall as many of the sentences as possible the next day in class.

What/How questions

To elicit WH– questions from your students, try mumbling or garbling different kinds of information, so that students have to ask: "Who did it?" "What?" "Where?" "When?" "Why?" and "How?" Or tape statements in a noisy environment where it is quite possible that students would not be able to hear every word spoken and would need to ask WH– questions.

To practice the language function of clarification, try the duplicatable worksheet on the back of *Picture 11* relating WH– questions to lifeskills. If you wish to simplify the exercise, try using fewer question forms and fewer verb tenses. The exercise in written form will help students focus on grammatical forms, but they should also practice the exercise orally as a question-answer drill, without their papers.

Answer Key

1. How much is the rent?
2. Where is it? or Where is your other building?
3. How many bedrooms does it have?
4. When will it be ready?
5. Why is it cheaper?
6. How long?
7. Whom should I talk to?

Inside an Apartment

Differences

(Circled in *bottom* picture, left to right)

1. curtain rod bent   **2.** faucet dripping   **3.** cabinet handle broken   **4.** no bottom stove drawer **5.** head turned   **6.** sleeve shorter   **7.** cabinet handle on right missing   **8.** different refrigerator style (or model)

STUDENTS SHOULD DESCRIBE CHANGES IN *BOTTOM* PICTURE. See pp. 1–3 for suggestions on implementation in beginning, intermediate, and advanced classes.

Context Questions

Let students participate with you in creating a story from this picture. Many of the questions below are open-ended—there is no one right answer—in order to encourage student involvement. Some questions depend on interpretation of clues within the picture, to encourage active thinking and attention to detail.

All questions are intended as guides only. You may think of other ways of phrasing them for your students. Or you may think of other questions.

Class discussion resulting from such questions will give you a chance to informally assess actual student performance in various language skills and lifeskills, with an eye to developing appropriate follow-up materials for the picture. (See pp. 3–4 for more details.)

FOLD PAPERS TO LOOK AT THE *BOTTOM* PICTURE ONLY.
- Where are these people? Are they living there now? Why do you think so?
- Who are these people? What is their relationship to each other?
- What are the men talking about? What are they thinking about?
- What are the women talking about? What are they thinking about?
- Do you think they want to live there? Why do you think so?
- Would you like to live there? Why or why not?

Language Functions

Language functions describe what people *do* with the language when they interact with each other.

Through structured dialogs, dialog development activities, and creative role play, we can give our students practice using the language in these different ways in situations that are important for their lives. Check the Table of Activities and Exercises for Language Development (following the Table of Contents), for dialog activities found in this book.

Some functions appropriate to the bottom picture are listed below. You may think of others. The examples given for each function are intended to stimulate your thinking. Reword them as necessary to fit your region of the country, the abilities of your students, and your particular lesson. (See pp. 4–5 for more details.)

Asking for information: "How much did you say the rent is?"

Giving information: "It's $_____ a month with a one-year lease."

Hedging: "Well, I don't know...That's a lot of money for a place like this."

Indirectly requesting changes by commenting on conditions: "Look at everything that needs fixing here. The _____ is bent/broken/missing/ leaking, and the refrigerator must be thirty years old."

Reassuring: "Oh, we'll be taking care of all that this weekend."

Lifeskills Extensions/ Further Language Development

See *Appendix 3*, pp. 104–08, for a list of specific lifeskills competencies and published materials that suggest activities appropriate for this picture context.

Look Again Pictures

12
Inside an Apartment

Can you find EIGHT differences between these pictures?

A Letter of Complaint

Write a letter to the landlord or manager of your apartment building. Tell him/her about:

1. Something that is leaking,
2. Something that is missing, and
3. Something that is broken in your apartment.

Choose the things you will write about from the lists on the board. Tell your landlord or manager about just <u>one</u> thing that is leaking, <u>one</u> thing that is missing, and <u>one</u> thing that is broken. Ask to have them fixed soon. Tell when you will be home this week, if s/he wants to talk to you.

_____
(Date)

_____
Dear (landlord's/manager's name)

_____

_____

_____

_____

_____

_____

_____

_____
(Your name)

_____
(Your apartment number)

_____
(Your telephone number)

Faucet-repair sequences using TPR*

Pictures of items in need of repair offer possibilities for activities using Total Physical Response (TPR), also known as Operations.

In a TPR activity, the teacher gives a series of sequential commands that present the steps needed to complete some task or process. During presentation, the teacher pantomimes the commands, using real objects if possible, or else pictures. Students then follow the same commands given by the teacher, pantomiming if necessary, first in groups, then singly. Next, students give the commands, or paraphrases of them, first by request (**T:** "Who remembers what comes next?"), then on an individual basis. Finally, after practicing the command sequence with the teacher, students practice with each other.

TPR sequences can include very simple tasks for beginning classes, or more complicated sequences with heavier vocabulary demands, perhaps describing an unfamiliar task or process. With unfamiliar tasks that cannot be completely demonstrated with objects in the classroom, photographs are a must—preferably, slides of you performing the task.

You could use the TPR sequence below for beginning classes:

Example

Drip, drip, drip. What's that?
Look in the shower. It's not there.
Look in the bathroom sink. It's not there.
Look under the refrigerator. It's not there.
Look in the kitchen sink. There it is!
The faucet is leaking.

Put your hand under the faucet.
Is the water hot?
No? Good, you're lucky.
Turn on the "cold" faucet.
Now turn it off.
Did the drip stop?
No? It's time to call the plumber/manager.

Calling the plumber or manager should be a separate sequence, with steps such as opening the phone book, finding the correct page, running your finger down the list of names until you locate the right one, picking up the telephone receiver, dialing the number, and the like.

For intermediate classes you could use this sequence:

Example

Uh-oh, the faucet's dripping again!
You have to fix it.

Look under the sink.
Find the water-supply valve.

Turn it off.
Get your toolbox and open it.
Take out your crescent wrench.
Find the nut on the faucet.
Put the wrench around the nut.
Tighten the wrench.
Turn it the same way that you turn on the water.
Oh no! It's stuck! Try again.
Still stuck!

Get the telephone book.
Open the yellow pages to the section labeled "P."
Find the name and number of a plumber.
Pick up the phone and dial the number.

With advanced classes, you can design TPR sequences to actually take students through all the steps of replacing a washer and the screw that holds it on the faucet. (Consult your local library or bookstore for the latest "how-to-fix-it" books with illustrations and step-by-step instructions.)

You will probably do best by having several shorter sequences describing various parts of the job, such as dismantling the faucet, collecting the damaged parts, matching them to new ones, and putting the faucet back together again. Slides or large photos *and* an actual faucet fixture are essential.

No matter which sequence you decide to use, you will probably find students with fix-it experience and inclination who may volunteer information or want to demonstrate. They can help you take your lesson further than you anticipated. Be alert to this possibility and help these students advance their own interests as they help you make slides or other lesson enrichments.

Writing a letter of complaint

Begin this exercise with a discussion of possible problems in an apartment that should be brought to the attention of the landlord or manager. Contrast leak<u>ing</u>, miss<u>ing</u>, brok<u>en</u>, and ask your students to help you answer these questions, making a list of questions and answers on the board.

- What could be leaking? (the shower, the toilet...what else?)

- What could be missing? (a stove part, a doorknob...what else?)

- What could be broken? (a window, a lock . . . what else?)

Use the duplicatable exercise on the back of *Picture 12* to give upper-beginning, intermediate, and advanced students practice in writing a letter of complaint to a landlord about three apartment problems they choose from the list on the board. Before students write, discuss as a class, "Should you sound angry in your letter? Why or why not?"

---

* See *Appendix 7*, pp. 111-12, for resource books on ESL teaching—notably, *Live Action English* and *Language Teaching Techniques*—that offer information on TPR.

Picture 12: Inside an Apartment

13 A Bank Line

Differences

(Circled in *bottom* picture, left to right)

1. cap instead of hat **2.** purse larger **3.** TV monitor smaller **4.** sign different **5.** no briefcase **6.** more hair on older man **7.** arms folded other way **8.** jacket closed

STUDENTS SHOULD DESCRIBE CHANGES IN *BOTTOM* PICTURE. See pp. 1–3 for suggestions on implementation in beginning, intermediate, and advanced classes.

Context Questions

Let students participate with you in creating a story from this picture. Many of the questions below are open-ended—there is no one right answer—in order to encourage student involvement. Some questions depend on interpretation of clues within the picture, to encourage active thinking and attention to detail.

All questions are intended as guides only. You may think of other ways of phrasing them for your students. Or you may think of other questions.

Class discussion resulting from such questions will give you a chance to informally assess actual student performance in various language skills and lifeskills, with an eye to developing appropriate follow-up materials for the picture. (See pp. 3–4 for more details.)

FOLD PAPERS TO LOOK AT THE *TOP* PICTURE ONLY.

- Where are these people? Why do you think so?
- How many of the people in the picture work there? What do they do there? What are they doing now? What are their job titles?
- How many people are being helped? What kinds of <u>transactions</u> could they be making right now?
- How many people are talking with other people? What kinds of <u>interactions</u> could they be having right now?
- How many people are waiting to be helped? What kinds of transactions could they be waiting to make?

Language Functions

Language functions describe what people *do* with the language when they interact with each other.

Through structured dialogs, dialog development activities, and creative role play, we can give our students practice using the language in these different ways in situations that are important for their lives. Check the Table of Activities and Exercises for Language Development (following the Table of Contents), for dialog activities found in this book.

Some functions appropriate to this picture are listed below. You may think of others. The examples given for each function are intended to stimulate your thinking. Reword them as necessary to fit your region of the country, the abilities of your students, and your particular lesson. (See pp. 4–5 for more details.)

Requesting routine service in a business transaction: "I'd like to cash a check...Will you update my savings interest, please?...I need a deposit slip."

Responding to a request for routine service: "May I have your bank card, ma'am/sir?...I'll need your savings record book...Here you are." (*Note*: Initial requests for routine service tend to be expressed straightforwardly, often as "I need..." or "I want..." [*not* in a demanding tone]. However, requests for non-routine or special service are more likely to begin, "Could I please...? Would you mind...?" or "Could you tell me how to...?")

Complaining: (Aloud to a friend, or to oneself): "I wish they would hurry up...Why are they so slow?...They ought to put more tellers on at lunchtime..."

13
A Bank Line

Can you find EIGHT differences between these pictures?

A Bank Form

FOR DEPOSIT TO THE ACCOUNT OF

BLG

Betty Luisa Garcia
2439 Elmore Ave. 661-0980
Oakland, CA 94612

DATE_____19_____

_____
SIGN HERE ONLY IF CASH RECEIVED FROM DEPOSIT

CASH	CURRENCY		
	COIN		
LIST CHECKS SINGLY			
TOTAL FROM OTHER SIDE			
TOTAL			
LESS CASH RECEIVED			
NET DEPOSIT			

USE OTHER SIDE FOR
ADDITIONAL LISTING

BE SURE EACH ITEM IS
PROPERLY ENDORSED

NFB

NATIONAL FUNCTIONAL BANK
Wilkins Office
899 Wilkins, Oakland, CA 94612

⑈080686321⑈0⑈0 2385100 629 ⑈ 00 31

Reading and Thinking

Read the questions below and think about the answers. If you are not sure of an answer, ask your teacher.

1. Is this form for putting money into the bank or taking it out?
2. Whose account is this form for?
3. What is the name of the bank?
4. Where is the bank?
5. What does "endorsed" mean? Find and circle this word on the form.

Reading and Writing

Betty Garcia wants to deposit her paycheck for $193.85 and withdraw $35.00 in cash. Her paycheck number is $\frac{63/1047}{1310}$. Fill out the form for her. Use today's date.

Making small talk with an acquaintance: "How've you been? I haven't seen you around lately...Did you see this article about...? ...How's the family?... How's the new job?... Did I tell you about our new computer?..."

Lifeskills Extensions

See *Appendix 3*, pp. 104–08, for a list of specific lifeskills competencies and published materials that suggest activities appropriate for this picture context.

Examining bank forms

With beginning classes, discuss the differences between checking and savings accounts. Use simplified banking literature if you can. Bring in sample checks, as well as deposit and withdrawal slips for both types of accounts, and have students practice filling them out according to your oral and written instructions. A duplicatable deposit-slip exercise is provided on the back of *Picture 13*.

Duplicate actual filled-out checks and slips, and have students examine them to determine which ones are filled out correctly or incorrectly. Extend the activity by giving an oral description of a slip, such as, "Mrs. Lee withdrew $50.00 from her account at First National on March 3rd." Students listen, then choose from copies of several withdrawal slips. All but one of these slips have one thing different: one was written by Mrs. Wing; another is for $15.00; another is from First Federal; another is for March 30th; another matches your description exactly. You can make the exercise easier by having fewer checks with more mistakes, or you can make it harder by having more checks and focusing on phonological (sound) differences, such as $15 vs. $50, March 3rd vs. March 30th, and the like.

Comparing services of banks and S&L (savings and loan) institutions

With intermediate and advanced classes, compare the services offered by banks and S&L institutions by using actual brochures, if they are available. Or make a list of banks and S&Ls in your area for pronunciation practice. Then give students the interest rates and methods of compounding interest featured for different types of savings accounts at these institutions.

Working with a specified amount of money, have students calculate the interest over a given time period for each type of account. Finally, discuss with your students the pros and cons of different kinds of accounts, such as high interest vs. lack of access to money, accrued interest vs. inflation, penalties for early withdrawal on some savings accounts, and the like.

Further Language Development

Listening comprehension and vocabulary*

Try this matching exercise with student pairs. **A** has a list of instructions similar to the list below; **B** has *Picture 13*. **A** reads to **B**:

Example

Put the number	**1**	*next to the*	woman with the curly black hair
	2		man with the cap
	3		security guard
	4		man who is partly bald
	5		female customer who is being helped
	6		male bank teller
	7		man with the handicap
	8		fourth person in line
	9		man in line with his arms crossed
	10		female bank teller

When **A** finishes, **B** describes the picture to **A** without looking at the instructions: "**1** is the woman with curly black hair. **2** is the man with the cap..."

A may look at the instructions to monitor **B**'s descriptions. When **B** finishes, **A** must describe the same scene without looking at the instructions. **B** may look at the instructions to monitor **A**'s descriptions.

Note: See *Additional Language Development Exercises*, pp. 95–97, for practice in contrasting "wish" and "hope" to accompany this picture.

---

*Thanks to Linda Cornejo, Alemany Community College Center, San Francisco.

Picture 13: A Bank Line

14 A Bank Desk

Class discussion resulting from such questions will give you a chance to informally assess actual student performance in various language skills and lifeskills, with an eye to developing appropriate follow-up materials for the picture. (See pp. 3–4 for more details.)

FOLD PAPERS TO LOOK AT THE *BOTTOM* PICTURE ONLY.

- Where are these people? Why do you think so?
- There's a young couple in the picture. Where are they? Do they look pleased or unhappy? Why do you think they feel that way?
- There's a handicapped person in the picture. Where is s/he? Does s/he look pleased or unhappy? Why do you think s/he feels that way?
- How many people in the picture work there? Why do you think so?
- What do the signs mean?

Language Functions

Language functions describe what people *do* with the language when they interact with each other.

Through structured dialogs, dialog development activities, and creative role play, we can give our students practice using the language in these different ways in situations that are important for their lives. Check the Table of Activities and Exercises for Language Development (following the Table of Contents), for dialog activities found in this book.

Some functions appropriate to this picture are listed below. You may think of others. The examples given for each function are intended to stimulate your thinking. Reword them as necessary to fit your region of the country, the abilities of your students, and your particular lesson. (See pp. 4–5 for more details.)

Congratulating: "Congratulations! You got the loan!"

Expressing pleasure: "Oh good! That's wonderful news!"

Expressing dismay: "Oh no! How did that happen? I can't understand what went wrong! Why is my account so mixed up?"

Calling attention to a particular place: "If you'll look at what it says right here... Talk to the man over there."

Indicating urgent need: "Mommy! I hafta GO!"

Requesting routine service in a business transaction: "I'd like to deposit some money/cash a check/join the Christmas Club."

Responding to a request for routine service: "Here you are, sir... Just a minute, let me get that form... Would you sign this, please?"

Differences

(Circled in *bottom* picture, left to right)

1. skirt shorter   **2.** hairstyle different   **3.** desk sign different   **4.** couple farther apart   **5.** hands on desk instead of in lap   **6.** collar different
7. earrings larger   **8.** hand pointing instead of curled

STUDENTS SHOULD DESCRIBE CHANGES IN *BOTTOM* PICTURE. See pp. 1–3 for suggestions on implementation in beginning, intermediate, and advanced classes.

Context Questions

Let students participate with you in creating a story from this picture. Many of the questions below are open-ended—there is no one right answer—in order to encourage student involvement. Some questions depend on interpretation of clues within the picture, to encourage active thinking and attention to detail.

All questions are intended as guides only. You may think of other ways of phrasing them for your students. Or you may think of other questions.

14
A Bank Desk

Can you find EIGHT differences between these pictures?

Character-Dialog Matching

Look at the <u>bottom</u> picture of the bank. Match each statement below to a person in the picture who could be saying it. Write the number of the statement on or near the person.

1. I just don't understand it! Why didn't my automatic paycheck deposit come through? My payroll plan is supposed to take care of this!

2. Mommeee! I hafta go to the bathroom! NOW!

3. I'd like to open a Christmas Club Savings Account.

4. Well, congratulations! Your application was approved for the full loan amount, and, as a veteran, Mr. Lee is entitled to the lower interest rate.

5. I don't think they have a public one here, honey.

6. My husband and I have been waiting for this for a long time!

7. If you'll look here, Ms. Williams, you'll see that your account first became overdrawn on this date. From that time on, an overdraft charge was added to every new check that you wrote on your account.

8. Certainly, sir. Let me get you a form to fill out.

9. Ask the man at the counter over there, Mrs. Sala. He can give you a key to the washroom.

10. That's wonderful! We really wanted to get that house!

Lifeskills Extensions

See *Appendix 3*, pp. 104–08, for a list of specific lifeskills competencies and published materials that suggest activities appropriate for this picture context.

Filling out bank forms

Go to banks and S&L (savings and loans) offices in your area and get brochures and application forms for opening a checking account, opening a savings account, opening a Christmas Club account, and applying for a loan.

In beginning and intermediate classes, work with filling out applications for different kinds of accounts with local banks.

Procedure: Choose a bank form that you want to work with, and duplicate it exactly. Copy the form on the bottom half of your master if the form is small; use a full page if it's large. On the top half of the master, or on another sheet, write or type a fictional description of a person. Mention all the information required by the form, as below:

Example

This is Kim Benson. She was born in _____ on _____ . Now she lives at _____ in _____ . She's lived there for _____ years. She's been working at _____ as a _____ for _____ years. She has charge accounts at _____ , (etc.). Now she's applying for a _____ . Here is her application form. Please fill it out for her.

Do this first exercise with your students, step by step. Then give them a second exercise with the same format but new information, to do by themselves or in discussion groups. Help as much as needed.

Reading bank/S&L brochures

With intermediate and advanced classes, use informational brochures from banks and S&Ls for reading exercises. In advanced classes, present text from brochures describing the same service at two different institutions. Ask students questions that will encourage comparison.

Further Language Development

Matching exercise to develop inferential reading skills

It is important in reading exercises to wean students away from constant use of dictionaries by encouraging them to guess at the meanings of unfamiliar words in context. Try the duplicatable worksheet on the back of *Picture 14* with intermediate students who may need a picture context to aid them in basic comprehension of written material. Or develop something similar to meet the needs and level of your class.

Ask students working in pairs to match statements on the worksheet to appropriate characters in *Picture 14*. Students should share one worksheet between them, but each person should have a copy of the picture. After eliminating the more obvious match-ups, each pair of students can discuss the others and decide on accurate identifications *without using dictionaries for word definitions*.

In full-class review of the exercise, be sure to give copies of the worksheet to all students so they can see troublesome phrases in print as you explain them. As you go over such terms as "overdraft charges" and "Christmas Club," keep the discussion within the context of the people and events in the picture. Discourage discussion about the phrases themselves or about any larger concepts the phrases may refer to. The primary thrust of this lesson is accurate character-dialog matching; study of words or phrases is secondary. A lesson on the new terms themselves might logically follow.

Answer Key

1. The woman at the left in the wheelchair. (*Clue*: She has a bank statement in her lap.)
2. The little boy at the right. (*Clue*: He is pulling his mother's sleeve for attention.)
3. The man in the striped shirt at the top of the picture. (*Clue:* He is standing at a window near the Christmas—Xmas—Club sign.)
4. The woman loan officer seated behind the desk at the bottom of the picture. (*Clue*: It says "Home Loans" on the sign on her desk.)
5. The mother of the little boy seated at the desk with the man on the phone. (*Clue*: She seems to be looking around for something.)
6. The woman seated at the loan officer's desk. (*Clue*: She appears to be with her husband and the dialog uses "my husband.")
7. The woman bank employee working with the customer in the wheelchair. (*Clue*: She is pointing at the customer's bank statement in an explaining manner.)
8. The bank employee behind the counter at the top of the picture. (*Clue*: He appears to be starting to get something for the customer at his window.)
9. The man holding the telephone seated behind the desk at the right. (*Clue*: He is gesturing toward the man behind the counter.)
10. The man seated at the loan officer's desk. (*Clue*: He appears to be getting a loan with his wife, and the dialog uses the plural "we.")

15 At an Airport

Differences

(Circled in *bottom* picture, left to right)

1. no sign on side of taxi   2. no shoulder bag
3. no man behind station wagon   4. porter going
other way   5. truck door open   6. terminal door
closed   7. boy standing instead of running   8. no
luggage in truck

STUDENTS SHOULD DESCRIBE CHANGES IN
BOTTOM PICTURE. See pp. 1–3 for suggestions on
implementation in beginning, intermediate, and advanced classes.

Context Questions

Let students participate with you in creating a story
from this picture. Many of the questions below are
open-ended—there is no one right answer—in order
to encourage student involvement. Some questions
depend on interpretation of clues within the picture,
to encourage active thinking and attention to detail.

All questions are intended as guides only. You may
think of other ways of phrasing them for your students. Or you may think of other questions.

Class discussion resulting from such questions will
give you a chance to informally assess actual student
performance in various language skills and lifeskills,
with an eye to developing appropriate follow-up materials for the picture. (See pp. 3–4 for more details.)

FOLD PAPERS TO LOOK AT THE *TOP* PICTURE
ONLY.
- Where are these people? Why do you think so?
- Which people seem to be in a hurry? Why do you
  think they are hurrying?
- Look at the woman in the crosswalk. Why does
  she have a dog with her? Why do you think so?
- The woman next to the taxi is holding a box with
  holes in it. What might be in the box? Why do you
  think so?
- How many kinds of transportation do you see?
  Name them.

Language Functions

Language functions describe what people *do* with the
language when they interact with each other.

Through structured dialogs, dialog development activities, and creative role play, we can give our students practice using the language in these different
ways in situations that are important for their lives.
Check the Table of Activities and Exercises for Language Development (following the Table of Contents),
for dialog activities found in this book.

Some functions appropriate to this picture are listed
below. You may think of others. The examples given
for each function are intended to stimulate your thinking. Reword them as necessary to fit your region of the
country, the abilities of your students, and your particular lesson. (See pp. 4–5 for more details.)

Greetings: "Hi Daddy/Uncle Roger! What did you
bring me?..." "Hey there, how's my boy?"

Asking for service information: "Hi, how much to
the Civic Center?... Oh, porter, do you check bags for
TYA Airlines?"

Giving service information: "That's not my dis-
trict—try the limo or the bus...Next one down,
ma'am. This is North-South Airlines."

Asking information of a stranger: "Excuse me, do
you know where the TYA ticket counter is?"

Giving information to a stranger: "Yes, I think it's
right through that door over there."

Lifeskills Extensions

See *Appendix 3*, pp. 104–08, for a list of specific lifeskills
competencies and published materials that suggest activities appropriate for this picture context.

Look Again Pictures

15
At an Airport

Can you find EIGHT differences between these pictures?

Writing a Letter to a Friend

You are visiting relatives in Seattle, Washington. Their address is: 4463 Belmont St., Seattle, WA 98145. Your friend Kim drove you to the airport. Kim is going to pick you up when you return.

Write a thank-you note to Kim and tell the date when you will return. Also write the name of the airport, the airline name, the flight number, and the arrival time.

_____

_____

_____

_____

_____

_____

_____

_____

Then address the envelope below to:

Kim Ho, 745 Eddy St., San Francisco, CA 94109

Put your name and your relatives' address in the space for the return address.

_____

_____

_____

_____

_____

_____

Comparing methods of transportation

Have students list the various methods of transportation to and from the nearest airport to some central point in the city (driven by a friend, personal car, public bus, airport bus from a private company, taxi, limousine, and the like). List whatever is appropriate in your area.

In discussing the pros and cons of methods listed, students should consider factors such as time necessary to reach the airport, frequency of service, cost of service (don't forget car-parking fees), and relative convenience (how much luggage you're carrying and how close to transportation sources you live).

Story problems

When transportation cost, time, and convenience factors have been discussed, present story problems featuring different characters who leave under different circumstances (time of departure, length of time away, amount of luggage, living in different parts of town). Have students determine which method of transportation to the airport is best for each circumstance.

Writing a letter

Upper-beginning, intermediate, and advanced students may need to use written communication with friends who assist them in getting to and from the airport. Use the duplicatable letter-writing exercise on the back of *Picture 15* to give students practice in:

- thanking a friend who has provided transportation to the airport;
- requesting return transportation; and
- providing specific day, airport, airline, flight number, and arrival-time information.

Or, develop something similar that fits the needs and level of your class. This exercise can be made more challenging by adding details about the trip, the relatives, and the like.

Further Language Development

Listening comprehension (true/false)*

Have beginning students fold their picture-pages so that they see the *top* picture only. They should also have a piece of scratch paper on which to write the answers to the exercise below. Read the following statements aloud while students mark **T** for true or **F** for false. (As this is a listening exercise, students should only *hear* the statements, not *see* them.)

1. This is a picture of a drugstore. **(F)**
2. There's a helicopter in the air. **(T)**
3. There's an airplane in the air. **(F)**
4. A porter is pulling a cart with some bags. **(F)**
5. There's a boat in this picture. **(F)**
6. There's a bus in this picture. **(T)**
7. A man is in the crosswalk with his dog. **(F)**

8. There aren't any children in the picture. **(F)**
9. One woman is pointing to the terminal and another is waving at the porter. **(T)**
10. Somebody is getting out of the limousine. **(F)**

Vocabulary/alphabet list contest**

With intermediate and advanced classes, put students in groups of three or four and have them select one person to be their recorder. Tell the groups to list as many words as they can that relate to the picture. Each word should begin with a different letter of the alphabet: **a**—airport, arrivals; **b**—bus, baggage, blind person; and so on. The words may be verbs or adjectives as well as nouns. Set a time limit. At the end, ask the recorder from each group to write the words on the board. The group that has the most words beginning with different letters wins. Then compare the similarities and differences among the lists.

Regular and irregular verbs

This picture is particularly rich in regular and irregular verbs. Have your intermediate and advanced students help you pick them out from the picture and practice them in their three basic forms.

Examples

REGULAR			IRREGULAR		
arrive	arrived	arrived	go	went	gone
walk	walked	walked	drive	drove	driven

Make affirmative and negative sentences and questions in different tenses about the picture to practice these verb forms.

Future or past tenses

With beginning classes, try the following verbal activity with your students:

Example (future)

You are (specified character in the picture). You are going on a trip. Where are you going? How long will you be gone? What are you going to do?

Example (past)

You just came back from a trip. Where did you go? How long were you gone? What did you do? Did you like it?

Note: See *Additional Language Development Exercises*, pp. 95–97 for practice in present perfect and past tenses, plus "if" and unreal conditional forms to accompany this picture.

---

*Thanks to Melanie O'Hare and Jo Egenes for ideas for the true/false listening comprehension exercise.

**Thanks to Janet Thornburg and Karen Bachelor de Garcia for the vocabulary list idea that I adapted for the alphabet contest.

16 Inside a Terminal

Differences

(Circled in *bottom* picture, left to right)

1. no snake on jacket 2. woman's hair longer
3. no tie 4. signs reversed 5. no suitcases
6. collar different 7. girl taller 8. numbers different

STUDENTS SHOULD DESCRIBE CHANGES IN *BOTTOM* PICTURE. See pp. 1–3 for suggestions on implementation in beginning, intermediate, and advanced classes.

Context Questions

Let students participate with you in creating a story from this picture. Many of the questions below are open-ended—there is no one right answer—in order to encourage student involvement. Some questions depend on interpretation of clues within the picture, to encourage attention to detail and active thinking.

All questions are intended as guides only. You may think of other ways of phrasing them for your students. Or you may think of other questions.

Class discussion resulting from such questions will give you a chance to informally assess actual student performance in various language skills and lifeskills, with an eye to developing appropriate follow-up materials for the picture. (See pp. 3–4 for more details.)

FOLD PAPERS TO LOOK AT THE *TOP* PICTURE ONLY.

- Where are these people? Why do you think so? (*Note*: It could be an air terminal, a bus terminal, or a train terminal.)
- There's a tall man bending over the counter. What do you think he's doing? Why do you think so?
- Look at the two people in the left foreground. Are they leaving on a trip or have they just arrived? What is the woman holding? (A tennis racket.) Why do you think so?
- There are four people talking together on the right. What do you think their relationship to each other is? Why do you think so?
- What does the little boy have on his leg? Why is he wearing it?
- In the background on the right, two people are walking through a gateway. The man is wearing something on his back. What is it? Why is he wearing it?

Language Functions

Language functions describe what people *do* with the language when they interact with each other.

Through structured dialogs, dialog development activities, and creative role play, we can give our students practice using the language in these different ways in situations that are important for their lives. Check the Table of Activities and Exercises for Language Development (following the Table of Contents), for dialog activities found in this book.

Some functions appropriate to this picture are listed below. You may think of others. The examples given for each function are intended to stimulate your thinking. Reword them as necessary to fit your region of the country, the abilities of your students, and your particular lesson. (See pp. 4–5 for more details.)

Bidding for attention from a parent: "MomMEE! I'm tired. Can I sit down?...Can I get a drink of water?... When's Grampa gonna come?"

Requesting reasonable action from a customer in a service encounter: "If you'll just sign the slip here, sir... and I'll need your telephone number below."

Complying with a reasonable request: "Okay... you want me to sign here?"

Making small talk while waiting for something: "Well, it won't be long now, huh?... Excited? I can

16
Inside a Terminal

ARRIVALS			DEPARTURES		
FROM:	TIME	GATE	TO:	TIME	GATE
TORONTO	10:30	26	NEW YORK	11:00	17
CHICAGO	11:15	37	SEATTLE	11:45	36
ATLANTA	11:20	22	DETROIT	12:30	41
LOS ANGELES	12:10	28	CHICAGO	1:20	24
NEW YORK	1:15	42	SAN DIEGO	2:30	22

TO GATES 32-45

Can you find EIGHT differences between these pictures?

DEPARTURES			ARRIVALS		
TO:	TIME	GATE	FROM:	TIME	GATE
NEW YORK	11:00	17	TORONTO	10:30	26
SEATTLE	11:45	36	CHICAGO	11:15	37
DETROIT	12:30	41	ATLANTA	11:20	22
CHICAGO	1:20	24	LOS ANGELES	12:10	28
SAN DIEGO	2:30	22	NEW YORK	1:15	42

TO GATES 35-42

Intonation Practice

In sections A, B, and C below, you will see three kinds of questions: Yes/No questions, *Wh-* questions, and "Or" questions. Read the explanation for each section. Then read the first sentence aloud, looking at the diagram. Practice reading the other sentences. Follow your teacher's examples.

A. In Yes/No questions, your voice rises at the end of the question:

1. Is this a grocery store?
2. Are people talking to each other?
3. Do some people have some luggage with them?
4. Did the children bring their dog with them?
5. Would you like to go on a trip?

B. In *Wh-* questions, your voice rises and then falls at the end of the question:

6. Who is the tallest person in the picture?
7. What is the little boy doing?
8. Where is the man with the backpack going?
9. When does the bus/plane/train leave for New York?
10. How do you find out where to meet an arriving passenger?

C. In "Or" questions, your voice rises before "or", and then rises and falls at the end of the question.

11. Is this an airport, or a bus station?
12. Are the mother and children traveling, or meeting someone?
13. Are the people with the luggage arriving, or departing?
14. Is the woman in the glasses talking, or listening?
15. Is the man behind the counter a passenger, or does he work here?

hardly wait!... And you know, dear, there was the nicest person sitting next to me, and before you know it we started talking and she told me that she..."

Lifeskills Extensions

See *Appendix 3*, pp. 104–08, for a list of specific lifeskills competencies and published materials that suggest activities appropriate for this picture context.

Reading schedules: Prepare questions about the schedules in the picture or about others that you bring to class.

Example
- When does the plane/train/bus to _____ _____ leave?
- From what gate?
- When does the plane/train/bus from _____ _____ arrive?
- At what gate?

Discussing baggage allowances for different kinds of travel: Compare the number of pieces, weight, and dimensions of baggage allowed for domestic air, rail, and bus travel. Also compare baggage allowances for domestic vs. overseas flights.

Comparing travel fares and costs: Compare costs of air, train, and bus travel to the same destinations. Consider group rates, other conditions for special rates, and such features as coach vs. sleeper rates (train), dining car vs. rest-stop meals (train/bus), nonstop vs. stop with layover and hotel (train/bus), and the like. You and your intermediate/advanced students can gather this information from ads, ticket offices, travel agents, and recent travelers.

Further Language Development

Student-monitored dictations

Dictations may take much less correction time if you have your students correct them. Self-correction makes the students responsible for paying attention to their own work, and builds self-monitoring skills in students who lack them. The key is training students to self-correct and to be attentive to the meaning of the text as well as to the listening, writing, and correcting procedures.

One approach to dictations is to give the same dictation on two successive days. On both days, you dictate and the students write, and then they dictate back to you and you write on the board. As you write, students correct their papers, using a different writing instrument from the one they used during the dictation (pencil instead of pen, or vice versa). Your writing on the board and the students' making their own corrections in a different color help both you and your students focus attention on problem areas.

The second day, after the dictations have been corrected, collect them and look them over. Count off only for mistakes that students did not find and correct themselves. Mistakes students have caught and corrected are not counted.

Picture 15: At an Airport, p. 62, and *Picture 16: Inside a Terminal* are good ones to use for dictations just before vacations because students are more likely to be traveling then and because holiday times are traditionally heavy travel times.

The following sample dictations can be used with high-beginning and intermediate classes in conjunction with *Pictures 15* or *16*.

Example (beginning)
Today is (day), the (date) of (month). It's the (first, second, etc.) day of the school week. Next week we don't have any school. It's vacation. Some people are going to travel. Others are going to stay here and work and rest.

What about you? What are you going to do next week?

Example (intermediate)
It's almost time for our _____ break. It's a good time to get away for a few days, and many people are planning trips. Some of them will fly, some will drive, and some will take the bus or train. Others aren't going anywhere because friends and family are coming to visit them here.

How about you? Are you planning something special for vacation? What would you like to do then?

Intonation practice: Yes/No, WH–, and "Or" questions

The duplicatable exercise on the back of *Picture 16* provides intonation practice for intermediate students. Explain the directions to the class, reading the first sentence in each section aloud as you write it on the board. Draw and explain the inflection diagrams. Provide verbal and diagrammed examples of other sentences in each section as needed.

Variations: More advanced students may wish to diagram the other sentences in each section.

When students demonstrate correct intonation of each kind of question, they should be encouraged to answer the questions. Discussion and practice can then focus on answer forms.

Student-generated Yes/No, WH–, and "Or" questions about *Picture 16* can provide additional practice intonation patterns and answer forms.

> **Note:** See *Additional Language Development Exercises*, pp. 95–97, for listening comprehension practice to accompany this picture.

17 Motor Vehicle Registration

Class discussion resulting from such questions will give you a chance to informally assess actual student performance in various language skills and lifeskills, with an eye to developing appropriate follow-up materials for the picture. (See pp. 3–4 for more details.)

FOLD PAPERS TO LOOK AT THE *TOP* PICTURE ONLY.

- Where are these people? Why do you think so?
- There's a line of people in the front of the picture. What are they waiting for? Why do you think so?
- The last man in line has something over his eye. What is it? Why is he wearing it? Why does he look so annoyed?
- There's an old<u>er</u> woman and a young man at the table on the left. Why are they standing there? (*Note:* "Old<u>er</u>" does not sound as old as "old." Compare: "She is an older woman" and "She is an old woman.")
- There's a man in back with a little boy. Why are they there? Why do you think so?
- Who is the young<u>est</u> person in the picture? Who is the old<u>est</u>? (Contrast young with young<u>er</u>, young<u>est</u>; old with old<u>er</u>, old<u>est</u>.)
- What is each person doing? Try to use a different verb for each person.

Language Functions

Language functions describe what people *do* with the language when they interact with each other.

Through structured dialogs, dialog development activities, and creative role play, we can give our students practice using the language in these different ways in situations that are important for their lives. Check the Table of Activities and Exercises for Language Development (following the Table of Contents), for dialog activities found in this book.

Some functions appropriate to this picture are listed below. You may think of others. The examples given for each function are intended to stimulate your thinking. Reword them as necessary to fit your region of the country, the abilities of your students, and your particular lesson. (See pp. 4–5 for more details.)

Giving instructions: "Here's your test form—you can fill it out at the table over there under the sign. When you're through, go stand in the line on your right."

Giving positive feedback: "Say, this is pretty good! You only missed one."

Responding to positive feedback: "Oh, that's a relief! Tests always make me nervous."

Completing a business transaction: "Okay, that'll be $12, sir."

Differences

(Circled in *bottom* picture, left to right)

1. no arrow   2. fewer buttons   3. more hair
4. man taller   5. no necklace (her blouse is not lower in the bottom picture: that's an optical illusion)
6. paper larger   7. sleeve longer   8. less hair (look again!)

STUDENTS SHOULD DESCRIBE CHANGES IN *BOTTOM* PICTURE. See pp. 1–3 for suggestions on implementation in beginning, intermediate, and advanced classes.

Context Questions

Let students participate with you in creating a story from this picture. Many of the questions below are open-ended—there is no one right answer—in order to encourage student involvement. Some questions depend on interpretation of clues within the picture, to encourage active thinking and attention to detail.

All questions are intended as guides only. You may think of other ways of phrasing them for your students. Or you may think of other questions.

17
Motor Vehicle Registration

Can you find EIGHT differences between these pictures?

Using Connectives: <u>AND</u>, <u>BUT</u>, <u>BECAUSE</u>, and <u>SO</u>

Below you will see ten pairs of sentences about the picture. Using a connective, write each pair together as one sentence. Choose the right connective from *and, but, because,* and *so.* The first three have been done as examples for you to follow.

1. These people are waiting in line. They have to get their driver's licenses.
   These people are waiting in line because they have
   to get their driver's licenses.

or *These people have to get their driver's licenses,*
   so they're waiting in line.

2. They don't like standing in line. They have to do it.
   They don't like standing in line, but they have to do it.

3. Some people are renewing their licenses. Others are getting them for the first time.
   Some people are renewing their licenses, and others
   are getting them for the first time.

4. The man in the suit wants to impress the woman in front of him. He's telling her about his expensive new car.

   _____

   _____

5. The woman is listening politely. She really isn't interested in the man or his car.

   _____

   _____

6. The man in the eyepatch is in a terrible mood. He just had a big fight with a friend.

   _____

   _____

7. The older woman has been renewing her license at this office for years. She always gets 100% on the written test.

   _____

   _____

8. Some clerks here start work at 7:30 A.M. They finish at 4:30 P.M.

   _____

   _____

9. Other clerks start at 9:30 A.M. They get off at 6:30 P.M.

   _____

   _____

10. The clerks don't take their breaks together. There are always a lot of them to help the people who come in.

    _____

    _____

Making small talk: (Trying to impress a member of the opposite sex): "Hi... What'd you think of the test?... Don't worry, I bet you did great!... Hey, you busy after this?... I just got a new Porsche... Wanna go for a ride?"

Note: The small talk above is presented as something the speaker *might* be saying; not what students *should* say in a similar situation. In the pictured situation, it is unclear what reaction the speaker will get. Discussing statements such as those above can be useful for establishing a context for questions such as, "Do you think the woman will want to talk to this man? Why or why not?" or "If a stranger approached you with these kinds of statements, what would you think? What would you say?" and "What would be an appropriate thing to say to someone you want to meet?"

Lifeskills Extensions

See *Appendix 3*, pp. 104–08, for a list of specific lifeskills competencies and published materials that suggest activities appropriate for this picture context.

Using driver's manuals

Good lifeskills material for reading comprehension exercises will come from your state driver's manual and from old forms of the written tests. Use information about hours and location of your local motor vehicle office to create answer–question exercises such as this one for beginning-level classes:

> T: "Here's the answer: 7 A.M. to 7 P.M. What's the question?" (What are the office hours at the Department of Motor Vehicles?)
> T: "Here's the answer: on Baker at Park St. What's the question?" (Where is the Department of Motor Vehicles?)

Interviewing students with new licenses

Students who have just received their driver's licenses or who are in the process of applying for them can be your best and most enthusiastic resources. Give these students the chance to be the "authorities" who answer other students' questions about license applications, driving tests, and the like. It's also helpful if you have all the relevant information in hand so that you can supplement the statements of the student "authorities," or question them further if they omit details.

In intermediate and advanced classes, have students practice making reported speech statements after interviewing each other about getting a license. For example, "What did Juana say about the written test?" "She said that it wasn't difficult."

Further Language Development

Vocabulary development

Most of the changes between the two pictures elicit various adjectives or adverbs of increase or decrease: larger paper, longer sleeve, taller man, more hair, less hair, and fewer buttons.

With beginning classes, you may want to focus on the semantic differences of longer and taller and practice using other examples. Do the same with the grammatical differences of less (with noncount nouns) and fewer (with count nouns). Note the particular usage of these two terms in your area. Are people where you live more likely to say "fewer buttons" or "less buttons" in describing the picture? (There is evidence that the use of fewer with count nouns is beginning to disappear from the language. However, its use is still considered correct.)

Using connectives

Intermediate and advanced students will probably not have much trouble with where to use and and but. However, the causal connectives, because and so, may cause difficulty for some groups, who may use them backwards: "I want to earn money because I have a job," and the like. You may want to spend more time working with statements of cause and effect if your students have these problems. Try the duplicatable exercise on the back of *Picture 17* for practice and an indication of students' strengths and weaknesses in using common connectives.

> *Answer Key*
> 4. so   5. but   6. because   7. and   8. and
> 9. and *or* so   10. so

If this exercise is easy for them, you can expand it by introducing other connectives in these groups:
- **and:** also, moreover, in addition, in addition to
- **but:** however, nevertheless, despite, in spite of
- **because:** due to, due to the fact that, because of
- **so:** therefore, consequently, thus, as a result

Notice that the grammar and/or punctuation of the sentence is affected in many cases.

> **Note:** See *Additional Language Development Exercises*, pp. 95–97, for practice with nouns used as modifiers to accompany this picture.

18 A Driving Test

Differences

(Circled in *bottom* picture, left to right)

1. fewer trees   2. station wagon instead of sedan
3. fewer doors   4. entrance nearer end of building
5. hand in pants pockets instead of jacket pocket
6. sign lower   7. more headlights   8. hair different

STUDENTS SHOULD DESCRIBE CHANGES IN *BOTTOM* PICTURE. See pp. 1–3 for suggestions on implementation in beginning, intermediate, and advanced classes.

Context Questions

Let students participate with you in creating a story from this picture. Many of the questions below are open-ended—there is no one right answer—in order to encourage student involvement. Some questions depend on interpretation of clues within the picture, to encourage active thinking and attention to detail.

All questions are intended as guides only. You may think of other ways of phrasing them for your students. Or you may think of other questions.

Class discussion resulting from such questions will give you a chance to informally assess actual student performance in various language skills and lifeskills, with an eye to developing appropriate follow-up materials for the picture. (See pp. 3–4 for more details.)

FOLD PAPERS TO LOOK AT THE *TOP* PICTURE ONLY.
- Where are these people? Why do you think so?
- Why are they there?
- There are two male figures in the middle of the picture. Who is the older one? Why do you think so? Who is the younger one?
- What do you think they are talking about?
- Is the younger one happy or unhappy? Why do you think he would feel that way?
- There's a girl with long dark hair sitting on the bench. How does she feel? Why do you think she would feel that way?
- Look at the other girl on the bench. What is she doing?
- There are two people looking out the window of the building. Who could they be? Why are they waiting?
- There are two people in the car marked "ABC Driving School." Why are they waiting?

Language Functions

Language functions describe what people *do* with the language when they interact with each other.

Through structured dialogs, dialog development activities, and creative role play, we can give our students practice using the language in these different ways in situations that are important for their lives. Check the Table of Activities and Exercises for Language Development (following the Table of Contents), for dialog activities found in this book.

Some functions appropriate to this picture are listed below. You may think of others. The examples given for each function are intended to stimulate your thinking. Reword them as necessary to fit your region of the country, the abilities of your students, and your particular lesson. (See pp. 4–5 for more details.)

Expressing anxiety: "Oohhh, I just *know* I'm going to flunk that test!"

Reassuring: "Now Wendy, you'll do *fine*. Just *relax*. It's not so hard. Really!"

Expressing curiosity: "I wonder if he passed it this time."

Giving negative information with mitigation: "I'm sorry, but I'm afraid I can't pass you this time."

Expressing disappointment: "Awwww gee..."

Asking for clarification: "What did I do wrong?"

18
A Driving Test

Can you find EIGHT differences between these pictures?

Review of Relative Clause Types

Look at the four examples below. Each example shows how two sentences are made into a complex sentence, using a relative clause. In each example, the relative clause is used in a different way. Go over these examples with your teacher. Then try to make similar complex sentences in exercises 1–8. All sentences are about picture 18.

a) The driving examiner is explaining the test.
   The test is given every day.

   The driving examiner is explaining the test, which is given everyday.

b) The examiner is explaining the test.
   The young man just took the test.

   The examiner is explaining the test, which the young man just took.

c) The examiner is explaining the test.
   The examiner has a reputation for being very difficult.

   The examiner, who has a reputation for being very difficult, is explaining the test.

d) The examiner is explaining the test.
   Many people try to avoid the examiner.

   The examiner, who (m) many people try to avoid, is explaining the test.

1. (type a) The woman on the right is trying to reassure her friend.
   The friend is about to take the test for the first time.

   _____

2. (type b) The woman on the right is trying to reassure her friend.
   Everybody has been helping her friend.

   _____

3. (type c) The woman on the right is trying to reassure her friend.
   The woman on the right passed the test last year.

   _____

4. (type d) The woman on the right is trying to reassure her friend.
   Everybody likes the woman on the right.

   _____

5. The Department of Motor Vehicles gives driving tests.
   The driving tests are necessary to get a driver's license.

   _____

6. The Department of Motor Vehicles gives driving tests.
   The Department of Motor Vehicles is a very busy place.

   _____

7. The Department of Motor Vehicles gives driving tests.
   Everybody fears driving tests.

   _____

8. The Department of Motor Vehicles gives driving tests.
   You can see the Department of Motor Vehicles in the picture.

   _____

Encouraging: "Take some more lessons and try again next month."

Expressing impatience: "This guy is taking all day with that kid. I wish he'd hurry up."

Lifeskills Extensions

See *Appendix 3*, pp. 104–08, for a list of specific lifeskills competencies and published materials that suggest activities appropriate for this picture context.

See the *Lifeskills Extensions* section for *Picture 17: Motor Vehicle Registration*, p. 70, for suggested activities relating to driver's permits and licenses.

Discussing consumer-related topics

Picture 18 can motivate previously reticent students through a discussion of cars and such topics as:

1. Naming the *kinds* (not *makes*) of vehicles pictured, such as two-door and four-door sedans, station wagon, van, truck, and the names of other kinds of cars not pictured. (Why are there so many kinds of cars?)
2. Naming *parts* of cars pictured that may need future repairs, such as tires going flat, headlights burning out, windows, door handles, rear-view mirrors or antennas getting broken, fenders or bumpers getting dented, and the like. (What parts are least/more/most expensive to fix?)
3. Discussing *new* vs. *used* cars in the context of cost, financing, condition, warranty, insurance, maintenance, needs, wants, and the like. (Why is buying a car so complex?)
4. Dealing with car-related *problems*, such as locking the keys in your car, having the car towed, getting stopped by a police officer, hitting another car, getting hit by another car. (What to do.)

Further Language Development

Listening comprehension*

The following exercise for intermediate and advanced classes is designed to help students determine the time expressed in a statement.

Example

Put this list of words and phrases on the board for students to copy, one word or phrase on each line:

- before, up to now, later, all the time, right now, immediately before.

Then read this text aloud to the students:

"These words and phrases all indicate different times that an action can take place. Repeat them after me and tell me what they mean. (Read and discuss list on board.) Now look at *Picture 18* and listen to the sentence that I will read. What time does the sentence express?

"Mark the number of the sentence next to the word or phrase on your paper that indicates the time expressed by that sentence.

1. The Motor Vehicles Office is always busy.
2. He should've been more careful.
3. She must be a nervous driver.
4. He tried to drive carefully.
5. He's been working at the Motor Vehicles Office for ten years.
6. He's just driven in.
7. She'll be glad when the test is over.
8. It's open six days a week.
9. He's explaining the problem.
10. He's been explaining the problem.
11. He's going to explain the problem.
12. He must've explained the problem."

Students are not to read the numbered sentences, only to hear them and write sentence numbers next to the appropriate words or phrases they have copied from the board. Here are the answers: before (2, **4**, **12**), up to now (5, 10), later (7, 11), all the time (1, 3, 8), right now (9), immediately before (6).

Review of relative clause types

The duplicatable exercise on the back of *Picture 18* is designed for high-intermediate and advanced students. Please note that it is not an appropriate exercise for the introduction of relative clauses. When used with students who have already had some practice with relative clause types, the exercise will demonstrate ways in which sentences may be joined by relative clauses at the subject and object positions, and provide additional practice.

Usually types **a** and **c** are most quickly learned and used. Types **b** and **d** are generally more difficult for students to grasp. The exercise may help you to assess students' current competence and where to begin teaching. Then you can develop relative clause exercises based on this model that match the needs and level of your students, for use with *Picture 18* and others.

Note: See *Additional Language Development Exercises*, pp. 95–97, for the Answer Key to accompany the duplicatable exercise on the back of this picture.

Thanks to Melanie O'Hare for this listening comprehension exercise.

Picture 18: A Driving Test

77

19 A Furniture Store

performance in various language skills and lifeskills, with an eye to developing appropriate follow-up materials for the picture. (See pp. 3–4 for more details.)

FOLD PAPERS TO LOOK AT THE *TOP* PICTURE ONLY.

- Where are these people? Why do you think so?
- What is the older girl doing? Where is she?
- What is the younger girl doing? Where is she?
- What is the older woman doing? Where is she?
- What is the younger woman doing? Where is she?
- What is the older man wearing in his ear? Why is he wearing it?
- Look at his face. How do you think he feels right now?
- What is he probably saying? Why do you think so?
- What are the youngest people in the picture doing?
- Are they having a good time? Why do you think so?
- Should they be doing what they're doing? What should they do?
- One person in the picture is a salesman. Which person do you think it is? Why do you think so?
- What is the relationship of all the other people in the picture?

Differences

(Circled in *bottom* picture, left to right)

1. TV larger   **2.** rug round instead of square
3. picture frame smaller or narrower   **4.** no sweater on man   **5.** no rug   **6.** salesman taller   **7.** girl's socks shorter   **8.** no wooden chairs

STUDENTS SHOULD DESCRIBE CHANGES IN *BOTTOM* PICTURE. See pp. 1–3 for suggestions on implementation in beginning, intermediate, and advanced classes.

Context Questions

Let students participate with you in creating a story from this picture. Many of the questions below are open-ended—there is no one right answer—in order to encourage student involvement. Some questions depend on interpretation of clues within the picture, to encourage active thinking and attention to detail.

All questions are intended as guides only. You may think of other ways of phrasing them for your students. Or you may think of other questions.

Class discussion resulting from such questions will give you a chance to informally assess actual student

Language Functions

Language functions describe what people *do* with the language when they interact with each other.

Through structured dialogs, dialog development activities, and creative role play, we can give our students practice using the language in these different ways in situations that are important for their lives. Check the Table of Activities and Exercises for Language Development (following the Table of Contents), for dialog activities found in this book.

Some functions appropriate to this picture are listed below. You may think of others. The examples given for each function are intended to stimulate your thinking. Reword them as necessary to fit your region of the country, the abilities of your students, and your particular lesson. (See pp. 4–5 for more details.)

Offering an opinion: "I don't think this picture is as sharp as the other one. What do you think, dear?"

Attempting to persuade: "Now, we can give you an excellent deal on that model, with very reasonable terms..."

Expressing enthusiasm: "YAAAAAAAAAAAY!"

Bidding for attention: "Look at me, Gramps!"

Scolding: "Hey, you kids! Get off of there! Now!"

Look Again Pictures

19
A Furniture Store

Can you find EIGHT differences between these pictures?

True or False

1. These people are in a restaurant.

1. That's false. They're at a store.

2. There are eight people in the picture.

2. That's true.

3. The girl on the sofa is wearing a dress.

3. That's true.

4. There are three young children playing around.

4. That's false. There are two young children playing around.

5. There's a bed in the picture.

5. That's false. There isn't any bed.

6. The older woman is looking at the TV.

6. That's true.

7. The older man is looking at the TV, too.

7. That's false. He's looking at the children.

8. There are two pictures on the wall.

8. That's true.

Lifeskills Extensions

See *Appendix 3*, pp. 104–08, for a list of specific lifeskills competencies and published materials that suggest activities appropriate for this picture context.

Comparing prices

Bring in newspaper ads and mailers from local furniture or department stores; compare prices for the same kinds of furniture. Compare models with different features at different prices. Discuss what makes a good/better/best buy as compared to a cheap/cheaper/cheapest price.

Planning furniture needs

Draw stick figures of a family that has just moved to town on the board and introduce the family members. Describe the size of their living quarters and tell whether a stove and refrigerator are included. This family has absolutely *no* furniture. Have students (as a class, in small groups, or individually) make a list of the essential furniture and appliances that the family needs. Part of this information will be determined by the size and age of the family that you draw on the board, and what you decide is included in their kitchen.

Planning purchasing priorities

Have students imagine that this family has been loaned _____ dollars to set up housekeeping. (The amount of money should not be enough to cover all the essentials.) Using the list of furnishings compiled in the preceding activity, plus advertisements and other sources of prices that you and your students gather, help the class decide: What must the family get first? What can they wait to buy with their first paycheck? What are some low-cost sources of furniture? and so on.

Further Language Development

Vocabulary lists

With beginning and low-intermediate classes, give students a list mixing twenty to forty items of furniture, appliances, fixtures, and the like that would be found in different rooms of a house. Have students in groups categorize the furniture according to the room in which it would be found (some items might be found in more than one room).

With intermediate and advanced classes, have students list all the verbs they can find in *Picture 19*, such as jump, kneel, point. Students could call out the verbs to you as you write them on the board; or they could work in small groups for ten to fifteen minutes, then give their lists to you to write on the board and compare. You can also tell students to make up sentences using the verbs.

Writing*

With upper-beginning through advanced classes, begin a paragraph about the picture and have students finish it.

> *Example*
> Tom and Alice went to a department store last Saturday. They wanted to buy some furniture... (Students continue.)

With advanced classes, assign each student a character in *Picture 19* to write about. (You can select the character or let students choose.) Students must write *at least* eight different sentences about their character, and more if they can. Sentences should be short and simple.

Ask students to read their sentences aloud to the class and/or have you correct them. Then have students combine the statements into compound and complex sentences, revising and changing when necessary or desired.

As a final activity, have students write a story of a page or more about their character. (Stories will be better and easier to write if the sentence-writing and sentence-combining activities are done first.)

Student-directed true/false exercise**

For communication practice, put students in pairs. One is **A**, the other **B**. Give each student a copy of the duplicatable exercise on the back of *Picture 19* and be sure each one has a copy of the picture. The first time through the exercise, student **A** sees both the statement and the correct response. **A** reads the statement to **B**. **B** looks at the picture and responds, "That's true" or "That's false," and corrects the statement.

The second time through, students switch roles. Student **A** now looks at the picture and responds to the statement. **B** reads the statement, this time with the paper folded to make the exercise more challenging. **B** must listen to **A**'s response, look at the picture, and determine whether the response is correct, peeking at the answer only if necessary.

Thanks to Karen Bachelor de Garcia for the "begin a paragraph" writing exercise.
**Thanks to Linda Cornejo for the idea I adapted for this true/false exercise.*

The Credit Office of a Furniture Store

Differences

(Circled in *bottom* picture, left to right)

1. woman's hair <u>a little</u> longer   **2.** no pen   **3.** fewer papers   **4.** no nametag   **5.** hand pointing to different picture (hand seems to be closer to picture, too)   **6.** woman's hair <u>a lot</u> longer   **7.** "twins" instead of "singles"   **8.** bed wider

STUDENTS SHOULD DESCRIBE CHANGES IN *BOTTOM* PICTURE. See pp. 1–3 for suggestions on implementation in beginning, intermediate, and advanced classes.

Context Questions

Let students participate with you in creating a story from this picture. Many of the questions below are open-ended—there is no one right answer—in order to encourage student involvement. Some questions depend on interpretation of clues within the picture, to encourage active thinking and attention to detail.

All questions are intended as guides only. You may think of other ways of phrasing them for your students. Or you may think of other questions.

Class discussion resulting from such questions will give you a chance to informally assess actual student performance in various language skills and lifeskills, with an eye to developing appropriate follow-up materials for the picture. (See pp. 3–4 for more details.)

FOLD PAPERS TO LOOK AT THE *TOP* PICTURE ONLY.
- Where are these people? Why do you think so?
- Which ones are the salespeople? Which ones are the customers? Why do you think so?
- What's the relationship of the customers to each other? Why do you think so?
- Are they going to pay cash for their purchase? Why do you think they are or aren't?
- What could the salesman be saying?
- What could the male customer be signing?

Language Functions

Language functions describe what people *do* with the language when they interact with each other.

Through structured dialogs, dialog development activities, and creative role play, we can give our students practice using the language in these different ways in situations that are important for their lives. Check the Table of Activities and Exercises for Language Development (following the Table of Contents), for dialog activities found in this book.

Some functions appropriate to this picture are listed below. You may think of others. The examples given for each function are intended to stimulate your thinking. Reword them as necessary to fit your region of the country, the abilities of your students, and your particular lesson. (See pp. 4–5 for more details.)

Urging: "If you'll just sign here, sir... Listen, when your folks see that all set up in your bedroom, why, you'll love it. Take my word for it. And this is the last day of our sale..."

Hedging: "Well, I don't know... I'd like to think about it more..."

Asking for clarification: "Wait a minute, those are monthly charges. What's the *total* we'd be paying, with interest?"

Deliberately giving an unclear or confusing response: "This clause spells it all out right here, in black and white."

Lifeskills Extension and Language Development

Scrambled story

If you have an advanced class, one way to involve students more closely in a reading is to make a problem-solving exercise out of it—in this case by scrambling the paragraphs.

20
The Credit Office of a Furniture Store

Can you find EIGHT differences between these pictures?

Scrambled Story

Ron and Linda had been looking for a new bed for a long time, but everything was so expensive! Then, when Big Town Furniture had a sale, they found something they thought they liked.

The salesman told them they could buy the bed on time, and after looking over the terms of the contract, it seemed to Ron like a good thing to do. Linda wasn't so sure, but Ron said, "Look, honey, the monthly payments aren't that high and we can start sleeping better. My back hurts every morning from that saggy old bed we've got."

So Ron and Linda looked over the papers and signed them. "You're in luck," said the salesman. "We can deliver this the day after tomorrow." Ron and Linda went home happy, thinking about their new bed.

When they got home, the phone was ringing. It was Ron's mother. "We've got a big surprise for you," she said. "All the relatives chipped in to buy you two a new bed for Ron's birthday next week. Your brother is borrowing a truck to bring it over after work tomorrow."

Ron and Linda looked at each other. What an unexpected problem! They had just signed a contract to buy a new bed, and now they were getting another one as a present!

So Ron called his brother and explained the problem. "Oh boy," said his brother, "Now you're really in a pickle. Mom's been working on this surprise for months. She got all the aunts and uncles to chip in on buying this bed. Why don't you return the one you just bought?"

"Well, I can't return it, exactly, because they haven't delivered it yet. But we signed a contract. We're legally obligated to buy that bed . . . aren't we?"

"Hmm," said his brother. "I'm not sure, but I've got a friend in law school. Why don't we let her look at the contract and see what she says? She tells me that they talk about contracts a lot in her classes."

So Ron's brother called his friend, and they came over that night to look at the contract. "Let me look at the fine print," she said. "Sometimes they have a special clause . . . aha! Here it is!" And she read them the statement from the contract.

"I don't understand all those long words. What does it mean?" asked Ron.

"The special clause means that if you change your mind within seventy-two hours, you can cancel the contract," said the law student. "You bought the bed today, right? This clause in the contract means that you can go down there tomorrow and cancel the whole thing."

"That's wonderful!" said Linda. "That means we can have a new bed and not have to make time payments!"

"Yes, you're lucky this time," said the law student. "Some people think that every contract allows for a three-day cooling-off period, but that's not true. Some stores include a paragraph in their contracts, but they don't have to. This one did. You should always read the fine print just to be sure, and ask for explanations if you don't understand."

Make enough copies of the duplicatable story on the back of *Picture 20* for all the students in your class, *plus at least half again as many extras.* Cut the extras into paragraphs, and put each set of paragraphs into an envelope. Give one envelope to every two or three students. Students must empty the envelopes, read the paragraphs on the slips of paper, and arrange them in order.

When the groups of students finish ordering their paragraphs, check their work, indicating which paragraphs, if any, are misplaced. After the group work, give each student a copy of the uncut reading, for class discussion and questions.

The exercise is presented to show one language-development way of presenting lifeskills information. If the concepts of buying on time, legally binding contracts, and the seventy-two-hour grace period* are very new to your students, spend some time talking about them before beginning this exercise. Working with new ideas in an imperfectly mastered medium is a double load. Present the new ideas as thoroughly as possible, with pre-activity warm-up, followed by the exercise itself and then post-activity discussion.

Further Language Development

"I want" discussion/grammar/writing exercise

You can adapt this motivating one-day-sale exercise for use with your upper-beginning, intermediate, and advanced students. Make a list of twenty or so varied household appliances, fixtures, and furnishings, including a mirror, toilet, couch, bed, lamp, table, stove, and the like. (You may want to make this a class exercise and list on the board items that students suggest.) Then:

- go through the list for pronunciation and meaning, and
- make an introduction such as the following.

Example

"Did you know that I have a store? Yes. It's (your name)'s Store for Furniture, Appliances, and Fixtures. And today I'm having a very special sale. Today only, you can choose *any one* item on this list and buy it for only $10. That's right, the special price today is only $10.

BUT you can buy *only one* thing, and you have to tell me why you want to buy it. Okay? I'll give you a minute or two to think about it, and then I want you to tell me what one item you want the most and why you want it."

This exercise can be fun for students and of interest to you for what it reveals of your students' personal lives. One father said he wanted a mirror because his children had broken the one in his apartment and his landlord wanted him to replace it; one mother said she'd like a second toilet because she had so many small children to take care of!

Beginning classes will be able to say less than more advanced ones, but the "today only" $10 special seems to motivate even reticent beginners to say something about why they want a particular item.

You may want to make this purely a communicative exercise, or focus on grammatical forms appropriate for your class:

Example
- I <u>want to</u> buy _____ because _____ .
- I want _____ the most, because _____ .
- If I could buy anything from the list, I <u>would buy</u> _____ .
- I am <u>most interested in buying</u> _____ .
- _____ looks <u>most interesting</u> to me.

For intermediate and advanced students, the discussion could precede a writing assignment in which they describe in detail why they want a particular item and what they would do with it after they get it.

Pronunciation practice

For intermediate and advanced students, make sentences with words containing /l/ or /r/ in initial, medial, and final positions. Don't neglect consonant clusters*. Some words related to the picture that you could include are:

Example
/r/: <u>R</u>on, <u>r</u>ug, bo<u>rr</u>ow, a<u>rr</u>ange, fu<u>r</u>nitu<u>r</u>e, sto<u>r</u>e, c<u>r</u>edit, p<u>r</u>ice, f<u>r</u>iendly, cont<u>r</u>act, sta<u>r</u>t.
/l/: <u>L</u>inda, <u>l</u>ike, <u>l</u>end, a<u>ll</u>ow, co<u>ll</u>ect, insta<u>ll</u>ment, se<u>ll</u>, g<u>l</u>ad, p<u>l</u>an, p<u>l</u>eased, ab<u>l</u>e, doub<u>l</u>e, sing<u>l</u>e.

Discussion question for all levels

What happens if you don't keep up the time payments on something you've purchased on the installment plan?

Note: According to the San Francisco Office of Consumer Affairs, the three-day grace period for changing one's mind about a contract is mandatory *only* for door-to-door sales. Businesses selling from a fixed place of business are not required to allow this period, although many of them do.

---

*See *Appendix 6*, pp. 111–12, for resource books on teaching consonant clusters—notably, *Consonants Sound Easy!, Initial Clusters Sound Easy!*, and *Final Clusters Sound Easy.*

Picture 20: The Credit Office of a Furniture Store

21 School Registration

Differences

(Circled in *bottom* picture, left to right)

1. no toy car 2. skirt longer 3. no telephone
4. no suspenders 5. girl's hair straight instead of curly 6. boat instead of plane 7. typewriter larger 8. stripes going the other way

STUDENTS SHOULD DESCRIBE CHANGES IN *BOTTOM* PICTURE. See pp. 1–3 for suggestions on implementation in beginning, intermediate, and advanced classes.

Context Questions

Let students participate with you in creating a story from this picture. Many of the questions below are open-ended—there is no one right answer—in order to encourage student involvement. Some questions depend on interpretation of clues within the picture, to encourage active thinking and attention to detail.

All questions are intended as guides only. You may think of other ways of phrasing them for your students. Or you may think of other questions.

Class discussion resulting from such questions will give you a chance to informally assess actual student performance in various language skills and lifeskills,

with an eye to developing appropriate follow-up materials for the picture. (See pp. 3–4 for more details.)

FOLD PAPERS TO LOOK AT THE *TOP* PICTURE ONLY.

- Where are these people? Why do you think so?
- What time does the clock say? Is that A.M. or P.M.? Why do you think so?
- How many adults are in the picture?
- How many of those adults work there? Why do you think so?
- What is each adult doing?
- How many children are there? How old do you think the oldest is? How old do you think the youngest is?
- What is each child doing?

Language Functions

Language functions describe what people *do* with the language when they interact with each other.

Through structured dialogs, dialog development activities, and creative role play, we can give our students practice using the language in these different ways in situations that are important for their lives. Check the Table of Activities and Exercises for Language Development (following the Table of Contents), for dialog activities found in this book.

Some functions appropriate to this picture are listed below. You may think of others. The examples given for each function are intended to stimulate your thinking. Reword them as necessary to fit your region of the country, the abilities of your students, and your particular lesson. (See pp. 4–5 for more details.)

Directing a familiar: "Shhh, Carlos! We just have to wait, now!"

Expressing impatience: "Wanna go PLAY!"

Requesting routine service in a business transaction: "Hello. We've just moved here and I need to enroll my son in kindergarten."

Responding to a request for routine service: "If you'll just fill out this form, I'll see when our counselor will be free."

Asking for a stranger's attention/making a reasonable request: (If man is a parent): "Excuse me, I can't find my daughter's teacher on this list. Can you help me?"

Asking for a co-worker's attention/making a reasonable request: (If man is a teacher or counselor): "Say Millie, what are we doing about the X2N forms?"

Expressing enthusiasm: "VROOOOOOOOM!"

Bidding to join in the action: "Hey, I saw that on TV last night!... Wow! My aunt/uncle flies/works on one just like that!"

21
School Registration

Can you find EIGHT differences between these pictures?

How Far Will He Go?

This is the office of an elementary school. The woman at the counter is going to register her five- _____ old in kindergarten. He's about to start on a long school career.
(1)

After kindergarten, he'll have six years of elementary and intermediate school, from first _____ sixth grades. Then comes middle school, grades seven, eight, and sometimes
(2)
_____. After that is high school, through grade twelve.
(3)

A high school _____, which shows that you have graduated from twelfth grade, is
(4)
necessary _____ most jobs. Many specialized, well-paying jobs also require a college
(5)
diploma, an _____ (two years) or a B.A. or B.S. (four years). There are technical schools,
(6)
_____, with vocational courses leading to special diplomas.
(7)

It's also possible _____ continue in the university to get an M.A. or M.S. degree,
(8)
_____ a Ph.D. Some specialized work requires these advanced degrees. Some professions
(9)
have _____ degrees of their own, such as the LL.B. and the LL.D. for a lawyer _____ the
(10)   (11)
M.D. for a doctor.

How far will this little boy _____ in school? It's up to him. His mother hopes that
(12)
he will go very, very far.

Lifeskills Extensions

See *Appendix 3*, pp. 104–08, for a list of specific lifeskills competencies and published materials that suggest activities appropriate for this picture context.

Teaching how to communicate with local schools

You may be able to perform a real service to your adult students who are parents, as well as to the schools their children attend. Contact those schools and find out some of their specific communication problems with ESL parents, and get some of the schools' standard teacher-parent communication forms. Encourage adult students with school-age children to talk to you about things they don't understand concerning their children's school, and to bring you forms they don't understand. Using their forms as a starting point, together with the information and forms you have obtained from the schools, construct lessons designed to make school/teacher-parent interactions comprehensible to your students. (See also the "Reading and responding to a letter from school" activity, *Picture 22*, p. 93.)

Further Language Development

Cloze dictation

The duplicatable cloze worksheet on the back of *Picture 21* on the American school system can be used with intermediate classes, and can be modified for advanced classes (with more words deleted). Give students the printed exercise; read the full script aloud while they read along and fill in the missing words.

Answer Key

1. year- **2.** to **3.** nine **4.** diploma **5.** for
6. A.A. **7.** too **8.** to **9.** or **10.** advanced
11. and **12.** go

Note: The information in this exercise may give rise to student questions. If your students are not familiar with the subject matter, some orientation to the American school system and the names and meanings of diplomas and degrees should precede use of the worksheet.

Listening comprehension (listen and write/draw)*

The following exercises can be used with *Picture 21* and/or can be adapted for use with other pictures in this book.

Beginning classes will need to know these words: typewriter, calendar, watch, tee shirt, banana. They'll need to perform these actions: write, circle, put, make, draw. Students should fold their papers to look at the top picture only. You read the commands aloud while students perform.

Example
1. Write your first name on the typewriter.
2. Circle the number "16" on the calendar.
3. Put a hat on the man's head.
4. Make a watch on the girl's right arm.
5. Draw a banana in the man's right hand.
6. Write your last name on the girl's tee shirt.
7. Circle the telephone.
8. Write your phone number on the man's paper.

Advanced classes can do a variation of the same exercise, as follows.

Example
1. Draw two bracelets on the arm of the mother in the business suit.
2. Put stripes on her son's shirt.
3. Find the child who looks the most irritated, and change his angry expression to a happy one.
4. Put glasses on his mother.
5. Move the clock ten minutes ahead.
6. Put polka dots on the blouse of the woman at the typewriter.
7. Make her typewriter dark.
8. Put earrings on the clerk at the counter.
9. Draw a beard on the oldest male.
10. Draw a vest on him, too.
11. Put freckles on the boy with glasses.
12. Change the pattern of his shirt to plaid.
13. Draw a doll on top of the toy car.
14. Make the socks longer on both little boys.
15. Make their pants darker, too.
16. Put the name of this month in very small letters at the top of the calendar.
17. Put the number "1" in the place on the calendar where this month really starts.
18. Write the name of our school between the clock and the calendar.

Intermediate classes should be able to complete a modified version of either the beginning or the advanced exercise.

Thanks to Melanie O'Hare for the first listening comprehension exercises that inspired me to write the second.

A Parent-Teacher Conference*

Differences

(Circled in *bottom* picture, left to right)

1. fewer books **2.** more flowers **3.** list shorter or fewer names **4.** man leaning forward instead of back **5.** no picture **6.** chair legs thicker **7.** girl's shirt outside her pants (that's why we can't see her belt!) **8.** rabbit's ear bent

STUDENTS SHOULD DESCRIBE CHANGES IN *BOTTOM* PICTURE. See pp. 1–3 for suggestions on implementation in beginning, intermediate, and advanced classes.

Context Questions

Let students participate with you in creating a story from this picture. Many of the questions below are open-ended—there is no one right answer—in order to encourage student involvement. Some questions depend on interpretation of clues within the picture, to encourage active thinking and attention to detail.

All questions are intended as guides only. You may think of other ways of phrasing them for your students. Or you may think of other questions.

Class discussion resulting from such questions will give you a chance to informally assess actual student performance in various language skills and lifeskills, with an eye to developing appropriate follow-up materials for the picture. (See pp. 3–4 for more details.)

FOLD PAPERS TO LOOK AT THE *TOP* PICTURE ONLY.

- Where are these people? Why do you think so?
- Who is the woman behind the desk? Why do you think so?
- Who are the other people? Why do you think so?
- Why are they there? What are they talking about?
- Do you think all American parents come to talk to their children's teachers?

Language Functions

Language functions describe what people *do* with the language when they interact with each other.

Through structured dialogs, dialog development activities, and creative role play, we can give our students practice using the language in these different ways in situations that are important for their lives. Check the Table of Activities and Exercises for Language Development (following the Table of Contents), for dialog activities found in this book.

Some functions appropriate to this picture are listed below. You may think of others. The examples given for each function are intended to stimulate your thinking. Reword them as necessary to fit your region of the country, the abilities of your students, and your particular lesson. (See pp. 4–5 for more details.)

Giving a favorable report: "Both of them have been making such good progress!"

Giving an unfavorable report with positive emphasis: "They're such bright, active children, but they have trouble applying themselves."

Asking for clarification: "Oh, in what way? Can you give us some examples?"

Giving clarification: "Well, for instance, look at this..."

Calling for attention: "MomMEE... look what Jen is doing!"

Refusing attention: "Not now, dear. We're busy."

Lifeskills Extensions

See *Appendix 3*, pp. 104–08, for a list of specific lifeskills competencies and published materials that suggest activities appropriate for this picture context.

---

*Cultural point: In some cultures, parents *never* meet with their children's teachers unless something is terribly wrong. It's a good idea to stress that parent-teacher meetings in the United States are routine events held to promote better parent-teacher understanding for the benefit of the children.

22
A Parent-Teacher Conference

Can you find EIGHT differences between these pictures?

NAME _____ CLASS _____

BIG CITY SCHOOL DISTRICT
Giffitz Elementary School H.A.R. Ried, Principal
Parent-Teacher Meetings

Dear Parents,

At this time each year, we schedule individual sessions for you to meet with your children's teachers and discuss you children's progress. Meetings last approximately 20–30 minutes.

You have been scheduled to meet with _____ *Mrs. Marx* _____ ,
Room ____ *212* ____ , at ____ *5:30 P.M.* ____ on ____ *March 3* ____ to discuss the
progress of your child(ren), _____ *Linda* _____ .

Please fill out the form below and return it to us this week. Keep the top part as a reminder of your appointment.

If you have questions about the meetings, or wish to reschedule your appointment, please call me at 431.8283 between the hours of 9:00–11:30 A.M. or 1:00–4:30 P.M.

Sincerely,

C.O. Ping

C.O. Ping
Counselor

-- (TEAR HERE) --

Dear ____ *Mrs. Marx* ____ ,

(check one)

☑ a. I can meet with you at _____ *5:30 P.M.* _____ on _____ *March 3* _____
        to discuss the progress of _____ *Linda* _____ .

☐ b. I cannot meet with you at the time indicated above.
        A better time for me would be

_____   _____
        (Date)   (Time)

                    _____
                            (Signature)

Optional: _____
            (Telephone # and best time to call)

92

Using math in analysis and decision-making

One lifeskill that often needs improvement is the use of math in analysis and decision-making. The need for math is obvious in consumer lifeskills situations, such as making purchases, applying for credit, or understanding a bank account. But it also can be applied usefully in many other situations. The following exercise is for intermediate and advanced students. You read the script while the students listen, take notes, work problems, and answer the questions.

Example*

Parent Conferences

A teacher needs to have conferences with the parents of each of the thirty-two students in her class. She is having a parent conference right now. She has had five already today, and she has three more scheduled after this one.

- How many conferences is she going to have today, altogether? (**9**)
- She had seven conferences yesterday, but none before that. How many more conferences must she plan to have? (**16**).
- If she decides to have eight on each day, how many more days of conferences will she need to have? (**2**)
- How many conferences will she have in all? (**32**)

Further Language Development

Adjectives**

Like many other *LOOK AGAIN PICTURES*, *Picture 22* is rich with phenomena designed to elicit adjectives. Have students help you make a list of adjectives on the board (<u>young</u>, <u>busy</u>, <u>interested</u>—there are more than thirty); then ask students to make sentences using them.

Reading and responding to a letter from school

Note: This activity may be appropriate for high school ESL students as well as adults. In many immigrant families, the older school-age children do much of the interpreting for the parents. If your high school students are recently arrived and have younger brothers and sisters, work with this exercise may help them aid their parents.

Duplicate the "Parent-Teacher Meetings" letter to parents on the back of *Picture 22* for distribution to

---

*Thanks to Melanie O'Hare for the Parent Conferences math exercise.
**Thanks to Karen Bachelor de Garcia for the adjectives activity.

Picture 22: A Parent-Teacher Conference

your students. In lower-level classes, you will find it useful to have the letter on an overhead transparency as well, to aid you in pointing out to students where they can find answers to questions that you ask.

As a reading exercise: It is desirable for pairs or small groups to work through the handout together, to find the appropriate answers to the questions that you ask.

Beginning classes: You may want to start by making a simplified version of the handout for low beginners. At some point, however, it will be useful for students to use the letter in its present form and work through it with you. Beginning students should not have every word explained to them, but should learn where to look for the most important information and how to ask for clarification of what the letter says is expected of them.

Upper-beginning classes: It is not expected that students will understand every word in the letter, or that you should explain every last detail to them. If you first present the letter to the class, unexplained, and a set of simple questions such as those below, you will discover how well students can cope and where you should begin teaching.

Example
1. This letter is from
   a) a supermarket.
   b) the apartment manager.
   c) a school.
2. The letter is about
   a) paying some money for books.
   b) talking to your children's teacher.
   c) getting a job at a school.
3. The letter says
   a) you will have a meeting.
   b) you will have a party.
   c) you will see a movie.

(Your answer to question 3 will help you with questions 4–6.)

4. When? _____

5. Where? _____

6. You will talk to somebody. What's her name?
   _____

NOW STOP. SHOW YOUR PAPER TO YOUR TEACHER. YOUR TEACHER WILL TALK ABOUT THE ANSWERS WITH THE CLASS. THEN THE CLASS WILL TALK ABOUT THE QUESTIONS BELOW:

7. Maybe you can't go at the time in the letter. Then what do you do?
8. Maybe you can go at that time. What do you do?

Intermediate and advanced classes: Structured questions about the letter, such as those used with lower levels, are unnecessary. Make your own WH– questions about the content of the letter and present them in oral or written form to the students for discussion. They could be discussed as a small-group activity before the general class discussion.

As a writing exercise: *Beginning classes*: In low-beginning classes, it may be enough of a challenge for students to check the appropriate box and fill in the signature blank on the handout or a simplified version. Upper-beginners could be required to change the meeting and choose an alternate date and time to the one originally given and check the appropriate box.

Intermediate and advanced classes: This handout could be the beginning of a series of assignments on parent responses to notes initiated by a teacher, and parent-initiated notes to a teacher. Such assignments would require an increasingly less structured presentation by you as assignments progress. The first few might be preceded by dialogs or short readings to set the scene: notifying a teacher of a sick child, giving permission for participation in a field trip, responding to a request for parents' participation as classroom aides, and the like. Later assignments might simply begin: "Write a note to your child's teacher about . . ."

Pronunciation and listening discrimination

Picture 22 has been designed to include elements that represent all of the vowel *sounds* of Standard American English, represented in a slightly modified Smith-Trager orthography* below:

/iy/	"Jean," teacher
/i/	"Jim," listen, picture
/ey/	"Jane," names, paper, cage, vase
/e/	"Jen," belt, tell, desks, bent
/æ/	"Jan," man, rabbit, laugh, hand, pants
/a/	"John," sock
/ɔ/	daughter
/ow/	"Joan," show, globe
/u/	"-ook," look, cook, book(s) (also: woman)
/uw/	"June," school, room, shoe
/ə/	"-un," run, sun, fun (also: moustache, tongue, brother, mother, husband, son)
/ay/	wife
/aw/	flowers
/oy/	boy
/ir/	ear, earrings
/ehr/	chair, hair
/ahr/	stars
/or/	door
/ər/	world, shirt

Appendix 7, pp. 111-12, lists books and materials that will help you to develop the enormous potential of this phonological content through structured and communicative listening and pronunciation exercises.

If you have not already taken a course in the phonology of American English, you will find it tremendously helpful to do so.

---

* See *The PD's* by Trager and Henderson (*Appendix 7*, p. 111-12).

Additional Language Development Exercises

Picture 3: A Clothing Sale

Pronunciation

In the sound system of English, there are three ways to pronounce the final -s of plural nouns and third-person singular verbs in the simple present tense:

/s/ following voiceless consonants /p, t, k, f, Ө/*

laps	/ps/
pants	/ts/
backs	/ks/
wife's	/fs/
the Smiths	/Өs/
He shops	/ps/
She sits	/ts/
He looks	/ks/
She laughs	/fs/

/z/ following vowels and voiced consonants /b, d, g, l, m, n, r, v, ð/*

ties	/ayz/
jobs	/bz/
legs	/gz/
seams	/mz/
buttons	/nz/
sleeves	/vz/
He says	/ez/
She holds	/dz/
He kneels	/lz/
He frowns	/nz/
He measures	/rz/
She breathes	/ðz/

/ɨz/ following sibilants /s, z, š, č, j/*

glasses	/sɨz/
packages	/jɨz/
It advertises	/zɨz/
He wishes	/sɨz/
She watches	/cɨz/

You can use the words listed above as well as others suggested by the picture, for pronunciation exercises. Start with individual words, then put them in sentences. Students can repeat, then make their own.

Picture 4: Exchanges and Layaways

Pronunciation

In the sound system of English, there are three pronunciations of -ed in verbs in the past tense:

/t/ following voiceless consonants /p, k, f, s, š, č/*

shopped	/pt/
looked	/kt/
laughed	/ft/
dressed	/st/
wished	/št/
watched	/čt/

/d/ following vowels or voiced consonants /b, g, j, v, l, m, n, r, z, ð/*

carried	/iyd/
grabbed	/bd/
hugged	/gd/
exchanged	/jd/
saved	/vd/
seemed	/md/
explained	/nd/
cleared	/rd/
(dis)pleased	/zd/
breathed	/ðd/

/ɨd/ following /t/ and /d/*

waited	/tɨd/
needed	/dɨd/

You can use the words above, as well as others that come to mind when you look at *Picture 4* (or *Picture 3: A Clothing Sale*, p. 14), for pronunciation exercises: first as single words for students to repeat after you, then in sentences that students read or make up themselves.

Picture 5: Getting on the Bus

Simple present tense and frequency adverbs

This picture lends itself well to practice of the simple present tense using adverbs of frequency.

Example

X takes the bus five days a week.

Y often takes the same bus, but not always. S/he sometimes goes to work/school later.

Z almost never takes the bus, but today his/her car is being repaired.

If beginning classes have recently been learning and practicing the simple present tense, encourage students to make up their own sentences. They can use phrases such as "take the bus," "wait for the bus," and "go to school," with adverbs of frequency ("always," "never," "usually," and the like) and with time phrases such as "on Wednesdays," "on the weekend," and "every Friday." Give students one or two new adverbs in addition to the ones they already know. Encourage production of negative as well as affirmative statements, and of plural as well as singular subjects. Intermediate and advanced classes can do the same exercise, using more advanced vocabulary and both compound and complex sentences.

---

* I am using a modified Smith-Trager orthography. See *The PD's* by Trager and Henderson (*Appendix 7*, p. 111-12).

Scrambled sentences with simple present tense and frequency adverbs

(See instructions for using scrambled sentences in *Picture 1: A Coffee Shop*, p. 6). If you have enough workspace in your classroom, a variation is to write the words for each sentence on separate pieces of paper, put the slips for each sentence into an envelope, and place the envelopes in different areas of the classroom. Student groups can move from area to area, piecing the sentences together, then reshuffling the slips of paper for the next group.

Picture 8: A Supermarket Checkout Counter

Dialog development through paraphrase

In developing the ability to get along in interactions outside the classroom, students don't so much need to memorize dialogs as to have a sense of the variety of things they might say in a given situation. One way to work on developing this sense is with exercises to paraphrase dialogs. Begin with a dialog such as this:

Example
CUSTOMER: Can I cash a check here?
CLERK: Do you have a courtesy card with us?
CUSTOMER: No. How do I get one?
CLERK: Fill this out and give it to the manager.
CUSTOMER: Now, what about my groceries?
CLERK: I can take your check if you have a driver's license and a major credit card.
CUSTOMER: Can I cash my check for more than the amount of purchase?
CLERK: No, you need our courtesy card for that.

After having the students discuss and practice the dialog, dictate it line by line and have students write a paraphrase of each line. Then, have them work in pairs, writing their paraphrase on large sheets of newsprint. A paraphrase for the first customer line might be, "I need to cash a check" or "Do you cash checks?" For the first clerk line, it could be, "I need to see your check-cashing card," or "Only if you have a card with us," and so on. In lower-level classes, have students paraphrase only the first four lines; in upper classes, all eight.

After students have written their paraphrases on newsprint, post the sheets around the room for the class to study what each pair has written. Then comment on the appropriateness of the statements and on the grammatical form used (focus more on appropriateness). After practicing all the posted dialogs, students can role play the situation. Encourage them to say whatever comes to mind, but to try to follow the general theme.

Picture 13: A Bank Line

Contrast of "wish" and "hope"

Ask upper-intermediate and advanced students to imagine that each of the people in the picture is thinking about something that s/he wants to happen. They should try to say the thing each person is thinking in two ways—once using "wish" and once using "hope."

Point out that "wish" can be used to talk about present events (as well as past and future), and that "wish" requires a different grammatical form in the verb that follows it. That verb form looks like <u>past</u>, but is in fact the <u>subjunctive</u>.

- The security guard <u>wishes</u> he <u>had</u> another job. (not <u>has</u>)
- The teller <u>wishes</u> the bald man <u>would</u> hurry up. (not <u>will</u>)
- The man in the sunglasses <u>wishes</u> the line <u>weren't</u> so long. (not <u>isn't</u>)

Point out that "hope" cannot be used to talk about some events in the present—what one is hoping about often needs to be expressed in the future tense.

- The security guard <u>hopes</u> he <u>will</u> get another job.
- The teller <u>hopes</u> the bald man <u>will</u> hurry up.
- The man in the sunglasses <u>hopes</u> the line <u>will</u> be shorter soon. (*or* <u>won't</u> be so long soon)

Have students make sentences about the picture, or about themselves, using "wish" and "hope" with appropriate grammar.

Picture 15: At an Airport

Present perfect and past tenses

With intermediate and advanced classes, distribute a text like the one below. Students can respond both verbally and in writing.

Example
Have you gone on a trip recently? Where did you go? How long were you there? What did you do? Did you like it?

"If" and unreal conditional

To give students written practice with conditional forms, try an exercise like this:

Example
PLAN YOUR DREAM VACATION
This is a contest sponsored by DBB Travel Agency. Write an essay describing your dream vacation. You are limited to two weeks in one location, but you can go anywhere, with anybody, and do anything. Be as specific as you can, and answer the questions below. The writer of the best essay will win the vacation.

- If you could go anywhere in the world on vacation for two weeks, where would you go?

- If you could go any time of the year you wanted, when would you go?
- If you could take anyone with you, whom would you take?
- If you could do anything you wanted to there, what would you do?

Or, as another possibility, try this exercise—it's a bit more challenging:

Example

Imagine that you were to meet somebody at the airport whom you had never met.
- Who might this person be?
- How would you recognize him/her? (Visual description.)
- How would you tell him/her you were waiting? (White courtesy phone.)
- If s/he were handicapped, what would you do?
- Where would you take this person?
- Where would you tell him/her to stay?

Picture 16: Inside a Terminal

Listening comprehension*

With intermediate classes, read the statements below while students look at *Picture 16* and mark their responses on writing paper. Label the top picture **A** and the bottom one **B**.

After each statement, ask students to mark **A** if the statement is true only of *Picture A*, **B** if the statement is true only of *Picture B*, and **AB** if the statement is true of both pictures.

1. There's a mother with two children talking to an older woman. (**AB**)
2. The hair of the woman on the far left touches her shoulders. (**B**)
3. The man buying a ticket has a design on the back of his jacket. (**A**)
4. There's some luggage at the counter waiting to be weighed. (**A**)
5. The woman in glasses looks like she's in a good mood. (**AB**)
6. The man who's chatting with the woman isn't wearing a tie. (**B**)
7. The little boy has a brace on his leg. (**AB**)
8. The guy with the backpack is going to Gate 32. (**A**)

Variations: With beginning classes, make easier sentences with more basic vocabulary and no relative clauses. With advanced classes, make more complex

---

Thanks to Melanie O'Hare for this listening comprehension exercise.

sentences with more advanced vocabulary and make four choices possible: **A**, **B**, **AB**, or **0** (zero) when neither picture is applicable.

Picture 17: Motor Vehicle Registration

Nouns used as modifiers

Much of the technical vocabulary related to the *Picture 17* context consists of noun combinations. With intermediate and advanced classes, practice forming and pronouncing these combinations, noting the particular rules:
- It's an examination for your eyes – eye examination
- It's a book of regulations = regulation book
- It's the registration for cars – car registration

(*Note*: A plural noun loses its -s when it becomes a modifier, as in the example above.)

- It's a permit for a learner = learner's permit
- It's a license for a chauffeur = chauffeur's license
- It's a manual for drivers = drivers' manual

(*Note*: Human modifiers take a possessive 's or s', whereas nonhuman ones don't.)

Some combinations don't fit either of the two patterns:
- It's a test you take on the road = road test
- It's the date your license expires = expiration date

Picture 18: A Driving Test

The answer key below is for the duplicatable exercise on the back of *Picture 18*.

Answer Key

1. The woman on the right is trying to reassure her friend, who is about to take the test for the first time.
2. The woman on the right is trying to reassure her friend, who(m) everybody has been helping.
3. The woman on the right, who passed the test last year, is trying to reassure her friend.
4. The woman on the right, who(m) everybody likes, is trying to reassure her friend.
5. The Department of Motor Vehicles gives driving tests, which are necessary to get a driver's license.
6. The Department of Motor Vehicles, which is a very busy place, gives driving tests.
7. The Department of Motor Vehicles gives driving tests, which everybody fears.
8. The Department of Motor Vehicles, which you can see in the picture, gives driving tests.

Table of Appendices

Appendix 1:

Incorporating Lifeskills Content 101

Appendix 2:

Related Materials for Expanding Lifeskills Content 102

Appendix 3:

CASAS* Lifeskills competencies, *LOOK AGAIN PICTURES*,

and Related Materials 104

Appendix 4:

Using American Names 109

Appendix 5:

Information Gap Activities 109

Appendix 6:

Using Overhead Projectors and Transparencies 110

Appendix 7:

A Short List of Handy ESL References 111

*CASAS is an acronym for *California Adult Student Assessment System*.

1. Incorporating Lifeskills Content

Lifeskills (also known as "survival skills" or "coping skills") refer to those areas of knowledge and procedures that adults in the United States must understand and perform in order to participate fully in a community. Lifeskills include: dealing in the marketplace to best advantage; getting service from various institutions; coping with governmental bureaucracy; and so on.

In the past few years the most immediately important lifeskills have been defined much more clearly, thanks to the efforts of many professional groups throughout the country. *LOOK AGAIN PICTURES* refers specifically to the work of CASAS (California Adult Student Assessment System). A complete document outlining CASAS' work and services may be ordered from:

> CASAS
> San Diego Community College District
> 3249 Fordham
> San Diego, CA 92110

Also during the past few years, numerous textbooks and source materials have been published that focus on lifeskills for ESL and for basic education classes with application to ESL. *Appendix 2*, pp. 102–03, lists related materials for expanding lifeskills content, while *Appendix 3*, pp. 104–08, lists CASAS lifeskills competencies and appropriate lifeskills materials related to themes presented in *LOOK AGAIN PICTURES*. These lists are partial because new materials are appearing all the time.

Working with American lifeskills in ESL presents a rather different challenge from teaching English per se, as proficiency in one does not necessarily correspond to proficiency in the other. Some students with elementary and intermediate English proficiency may comprehend and perform some aspects of lifeskills quite well; others who have advanced language proficiency but who have arrived in the United States only recently know nothing at all about lifeskills in this culture. Within a single class of students at approximately the same linguistic level, there may be a wide range of lifeskills knowledge and ability.

How, then, to deal with this challenge? For starters, an ongoing assessment of "who knows what" is important with each lifeskill you cover. One kind of informal evaluation can develop from discussion of pictures such as the ones in this book. In *Picture 14: A Bank Desk*, for example (p. 58), a general discussion of what papers the couple might be reviewing can help you get a sense of what your students already know and where you should start.

You probably will find that some of your students seem to know a great deal. These students can help you explain new concepts to others in the class and can serve as leaders in group exercises involving filling out forms, or provide information about various lifeskills. The leaders may have stories to share with the class ("You say you just got your driver's license, Maria? What did you have to do to get it? . . . Sing Loo, what happened when you went to open a bank account?"), as well as questions of their own about the theme being discussed. Students with advanced lifeskills knowledge and ability will appreciate having special assignments to work on, while you do simpler exercises with the rest of the class.

In any case, it is important to: find out who knows what; acknowledge their skills and gain their agreement that what you're doing is important for the rest of the class; and engage their cooperation in helping you, or in working independently on another, more challenging, activity. Assure them that you will soon be going on to other activities that interest them.

In preparing lifeskills lessons, remember to go beyond the talking stage that occurs during your initial assessment. Give the students practice in filling out forms, finding relevant information, computing costs per unit, and so on. The books cited in *Appendix 2* and *Appendix 3* offer many useful examples, which you can adapt to your own situation.

2. Related Materials for Expanding Lifeskills Content*

Supplements or Main Texts

**A Conversation Book: English in Everyday Life.* Bks. I & II. By Carver and Fotinos. Englewood Cliffs, N.J.: Prentice-Hall, 1977. (High beginning-intermediate level.)

**English for Adult Competency.* Bks. I & II. By Keltner et al. Englewood Cliffs, N.J.: Prentice-Hall, 1981. (Beginning-intermediate level.)

Improving Aural Comprehension: Student's Workbook. By Morley. Ann Arbor: University of Michigan Press, 1972. (Beginning-intermediate-advanced level.)

Improving Aural Comprehension: Teacher's Book of Readings. By Morley. Ann Arbor: University of Michigan Press, 1972. (Beginning-intermediate-advanced level.)

***LifeSchool Beginning Classroom Modules: Lifeskills Literacy.* Binder 1: Consumer Economics; Binder 2: Health; Binder 3: Government and Law and Community Resources; Binder 4: Occupational Knowledge and Interpersonal Relations. Clovis, California, Adult School. Belmont, Ca.: Pitman Learning, 1981. (Beginning-intermediate ABE materials with an ESL component.)

**NHE Lifeskills Workbook.* Nos. I (1981) & II (1982). By DeFilippo and Walker. Reading, Mass.: Addison-Wesley, 1981, 1982. (Beginning-intermediate level.)

Notion by Notion. By Ferreira. Rowley, Mass.: Newbury House, 1981. (High beginning level.)

Side by Side: English Grammar through Guided Conversations. Bk. I. By Molinsky and Bliss. Englewood Cliffs, N.J.: Prentice-Hall, 1980. (Beginning level.)

Main Texts

Beyond the Classroom. By Cathcart and Strong. Rowley, Mass.: Newbury House, l983. (Low intermediate level.)

English That Works. Vols. I & II. By Savage et al. Glenview, Ill.: Scott Foresman, 1982. (Pre-vocational beginning level.)

Everyday English. Vols. I, IIA, IIB. By Prather, Quan, and Schurer. Hayward, Ca.: Alemany Press, 1980. (Absolute beginning level.)

It's Up to You. By Dresner et al. New York: Longman, 1980. (High intermediate vocational level.)

**Lifelines.* Nos. I-IV. By Foley and Pomann. New York: Regents Publishing Co., 1981. (Beginning-intermediate level.)

Lifestyles. Vols. I & II. By Kimbrough and Cardenas. New York: Longman, 1982. (Intermediate-advanced level.)

Speaking of Survival. By Freeman. New York: Oxford University Press, 1982. (High beginning-low intermediate level.)

Picture Sources

Conversational Survival Skills. By Hamel. Beverly Hills, Ca.: Easy Aids, 1981. (Duplicatable.)

Double Action Picture Cards. By Yedlin. Reading, Mass.: Addison-Wesley, 1981. (Large pictures on heavy cardboard.)

More Pictures That Teach Words. By Chaille. Beverly Hills, Ca.: Easy Aids, 1980. (Duplicatable.)

Necessary Words to Live By. By Hamel. Beverly Hills, Ca.: Easy Aids, 1980. (Duplicatable.)

Oxford Picture Dictionary of American English. By Parnwell. New York: Oxford University Press, 1978.

Practical Vocabulary Builder. By Liebowitz. Skokie, Ill.: National Textbook Co., 1983. (Duplicatable.)

The Vocabulary Builder. By Chaille. Beverly Hills, Ca.: Easy Aids, 1979. (Duplicatable.)

Vocabulary through Pictures. By Chaille. Beverly Hills, Ca.: Easy Aids, 1979. (Duplicatable.)

Teacher Idea Books

Communication-Starters and Other Activities for the ESL Classroom. By Olsen. Hayward, Ca.: Alemany Press, 1977. (Contains maps for duplication.)

---

*Appendix 3, pp. 104–08, cross-references the specific themes of these materials as they appear in specific pictures.
**Highly recommended as all-around sourcebooks/reference books for your lifeskills library.
***Also known as *The Clovis Modules* and *Project Class*. These detailed materials contain complete teaching plans plus black-line master sheets to duplicate and distribute to students.

Readers

No Cold Water Either. By Bodman and Lanzano. New York: Collier Macmillan, 1980. (Low intermediate level.)

No Hot Water Tonight. By Bodman and Lanzano. New York: Collier Macmillan, 1970. (Low intermediate level.)

**Read Right! Developing Survival Reading Skills.* By Chamot. New York: Minerva Books, 1982. (Very advanced level.)

The New Arrival. Book Two. By Kuntz. Hayward, Ca.: Alemany Press, 1982. (Beginning level.)

Workbooks for Secondary Special Education: Adaptable for Intermediate ESL

(All the titles below are available from Janus Book Publishers, 2501 Industrial Parkway West, Hayward, CA 94545.)

Banking Language. By Richey, 1980.

Be Ad-Wise: A Guide to Reading Ads. By Canario, 1981.

Becoming a Driver. By Grebel and Pogrund, 1981.

Be Credit-Wise: A Guide to Credit. By Schwartz, 1983.

Caring for Your Car. By Grebel and Pogrund, 1981.

Clothing Language. By Richey, 1979.

Credit Language. By Richey, 1980.

Don't Get Fired!: 13 Ways to Hold Your Job. By Anema, 1978.

Driver's License Language. By Richey, 1980.

Drugstore Language. By Richey, 1978.

Finding a Good Used Car. By Fletcher and Kelly, 1977.

Get Hired!: 13 Ways to Get a Job. By Anema, 1979.

Getting Around Cities and Towns. By Roderman, 1979.

Getting Help: A Guide to Community Services. By Chan, 1981.

Help!: First Steps to First Aid. By Canario and Mathias, 1980.

Hospital Jobs. By Schwartz, 1983.

Hospital Words. By Richey, 1983.

Hotel/Motel Jobs. By Schwartz and Budd, 1983.

Hotel/Motel Words. By Richey, 1983.

Insure Yourself: A Guide to Insurance. By Schwartz, 1983.

Janus Job Interview Guide. By Livingstone, 1977.

Janus Job Interview Kit. By Jew and Tong, 1976. (Contains photo cards, spirit masters, book of job information tickets, teacher's guide.)

Janus Job Planner. By Jew and Tong, 1976.

Job Application Language. By Richey, 1978.

Know Your Rights: A Guide to Consumer Protection. By Schwartz, 1983.

Make Your Money Grow: A Guide to Savings Plans. By Schwartz, 1983.

Master Your Money: A Guide to Budgeting. By Wilson, 1981.

Medical Language. By Richey, 1980.

More for Your Money: A Guide to Comparison Shopping. By Kelsey and Gundlach, 1981.

My Job Application File. By Kahn, Jew, and Tong, 1980.

Need A Doctor? By Lappin and Feinglass, 1981.

Pay by Check: A Guide to Checking Accounts. By Chan, 1981.

Reading and Following Directions. By Roderman, 1978.

Reading a Newspaper. By Larned and Randall, 1978.

Reading Schedules. By Roderman, 1978.

Restaurant Jobs. By Schwartz, 1983.

Restaurant Language. By Richey, 1978.

Restaurant Words. By Richey, 1978.

Sign Language. Books A-D. By Richey, 1976, 1977.

Store Jobs. By Schwartz and Budd, 1983.

Store Words. By Richey, 1983.

Supermarket Language. By Richey, 1978.

Time Cards and Paychecks. By Rand, 1981.

Using the Phone Book. By Gundlach and Kelsey, 1980.

Using the Want Ads. By Jew and Tandy, 1977.

**Highly recommended as all-around sourcebooks/reference books for your lifeskills library.*

3. CASAS* Lifeskills Competencies, *LOOK AGAIN PICTURES*, and Related Materials

Picture 1: A Coffee Shop

(CASAS 2.6.4: "The student will be able to demonstrate how to order restaurant food and leave an appropriate tip.")

Conversation Book, I, pp. 159–60.

English for Adult Competency, I, pp. 40–46; II, pp. 42–45.

Lifelines, I, pp. 45–49; II, pp. 45–49.

LifeSchool: Consumer Economics, pp. 475–538.

More Pictures That Teach Words, p. 16.

Necessary Words to Live By, p. 7.

NHE Lifeskills, I, pp. 53–54; II, p. 102.

Notion by Notion, II, pp. 32–33.

Practical Vocabulary Builder, pp. 14, 15.

Read Right! pp. 7–10.

Restaurant Language.

Side by Side, I, p. 120.

Vocabulary Builder, pp. 14, 15.

Picture 2: A Coffee Shop Kitchen

(CASAS 4.1: "The student will be able to demonstrate the ability to identify factors associated with applying for and maintaining a job."
CASAS 4.3: "...identify work-safety procedures required in selected occupations.")

Beyond the Classroom, pp. 102–20.

Conversational Survival Skills, pp. 3, 15.

Conversation Book, I, pp. 120–27; II, pp. 84–93.

English for Adult Competency, I, pp. 121–38; II, pp. 129–48.

English That Works, I & II.

Everyday English, I & IIB.

Get Hired!

It's Up to You.

Job Application Language.

Lifelines, I, pp. 11–19; II, pp. 11–19.

LifeSchool: Occupational Knowledge and Interpersonal Relations, pp. 1–292.

NHE Lifeskills, II, pp. 18–36, 47–65.

Read Right! pp. 61–76.

Speaking of Survival, pp. 82–96.

Using the Want Ads, pp. 25–36.

Picture 3: A Clothing Sale

Picture 4: Exchanges and Layaways

(CASAS 1.2: "The student will demonstrate the ability to apply the principles of comparison shopping in the selecting of goods and services."
CASAS 1.3: "...identify different purchasing methods for goods and services."
CASAS 1.5: "...interpret information associated with budgeting and expenditures."
CASAS 1.7: "...relate basic procedures for the care and upkeep of personal possessions.")

Be Ad-Wise, pp. 52–55.

Beyond the Classroom, pp. 176–91.

Clothing Language.

Conversation Book, I, pp. 87–93; II, pp. 28–37.

English for Adult Competency, I, pp. 103–20; II, pp. 113–27.

Everyday English, I & IIA.

Lifelines, I, pp. 51–59; II, pp. 51–59; III, pp. 43–49; IV, pp. 35–40.

LifeSchool: Consumer Economics, pp. 213–74, 345–410.

More for Your Money.

NHE Lifeskills, I, pp. 14–24.

Notion by Notion, pp. 18–19, 34–37.

Practical Vocabulary Builder, p. 12.

---

*CASAS is an acronym for *California Adult Student Assessment System*.

Read Right! pp. 30–43.

Speaking of Survival, pp. 162–76.

Vocabulary Builder, pp. 2–3.

Picture 5: Getting on the Bus

Picture 6: Riding on the Bus

(CASAS 2.2.1: "The student will be able to demonstrate the ability to ask for and give directions."
CASAS 2.2.2: "...recognize and utilize signs connected with transportation."
CASAS 2.2.4: "...interpret transportation schedules and calculate fares."
CASAS 2.2.5: "...use maps related to travel needs.")

Beyond the Classroom, pp. 81–85.

Communication-Starters, pp. 37–61.

Conversation Book, I, pp. 105–7, 111–12; II, pp. 17, 44, 56–57.

English for Adult Competency, I, pp. 68–72; II, pp. 74, 76, 79–82.

English That Works, II, pp. 42–83.

Everyday English, I & IIA.

Improving Aural Comprehension, pp. 95–142.

Lifelines, I, pp. 35–39, 71–74; II, pp. 35–39; III, pp. 35–42.

LifeSchool: Community Resources, pp. 113–76.

More Pictures That Teach Words, p. 18.

NHE Lifeskills, I, pp. 57–58.

Notion by Notion, pp. 14–15.

Read Right! pp. 50–56.

Side by Side, I, pp. 144–49.

Speaking of Survival, pp. 162–76.

Picture 7: A Supermarket Aisle

Picture 8: A Supermarket Checkout Counter

(CASAS 1.1.7: "The student will demonstrate the ability to interpret product container sizes."
CASAS 1.2.1: "...interpret advertisements, labels or charts to select the best buys for goods and services."

CASAS 1.2.4: "...compute unit pricing."
CASAS 1.6.1: "...interpret food packaging labels."
CASAS 3.5.1: "...interpret nutritional information from food labels."
CASAS 3.5.2: "...select what constitutes a balanced diet using the four basic food groups.")

Be Ad-Wise, pp. 50–59.

Beyond the Classroom, pp. 130–38.

Conversation Book, I, pp. 80–85; II, pp. 20–25.

English for Adult Competency, I, pp. 25–39, 44, 47–48; II, pp. 27–40, 47–49.

Everyday English, I & IIA.

Lifelines, I, pp. 41–44; II, pp. 41–44.

LifeSchool: Consumer Education, pp. 141–212.

More for Your Money.

More Pictures That Teach Words, p. 3.

Necessary Words to Live By, p. 8.

NHE Lifeskills, I, pp. 42–52; II, p. 101.

Notion by Notion, pp. 22–23.

Side by Side, I, pp. 118–19.

Speaking of Survival, pp. 146–59.

Supermarket Language.

Picture 9: A Clinic Waiting Room

Picture 10: Talking to the Doctor

(CASAS 2.5.1: "The student will demonstrate the ability to identify types of community services that provide emergency help."
CASAS 2.5.2: "...identify the application process for community services."
CASAS 2.5.3: "...locate medical and health services in the community."
CASAS 3.1: "...identify common ailments and seek appropriate medical assistance."
CASAS 3.2: "...interpret forms and information related to medical and dental care."
CASAS 3.3: "...identify and select appropriate medications."
CASAS 3.4.1: "...interpret product label warnings, signs, and symbols."
CASAS 3.6.1: "...demonstrate how to place emergency calls to a doctor, hospital, or for an ambulance.")

Beyond the Classroom, pp. 53–65, 121–25.

Conversation Book, I, pp. 130–47; II, pp. 104–20.

Drugstore Language.

English for Adult Competency, I, pp. 49–66; II, pp. 51–71.

Everyday English, I & IIB.

Getting Help, pp. 31–42.

Insure Yourself.

Lifelines, I, pp. 81–89; II, pp. 81–89; III, pp. 63–76; IV, pp. 55–68.

LifeSchool: Community Resources, pp. 285–340; *Health*, complete volume.

Medical Language.

More Pictures That Teach Words, p. 19.

Need a Doctor?

NHE Lifeskills, I, pp. 87–96; II, pp. 66–75.

Notion by Notion, pp. 66–67.

Practical Vocabulary Builder, pp. 7, 10.

Reading and Following Directions, pp. 58–59.

Read Right! pp. 77–84.

Side by Side, I, p. 91.

Speaking of Survival, pp. 2–31.

Vocabulary Builder, pp. 7, 10.

Picture 11: Outside an Apartment

Picture 12: Inside an Apartment

(CASAS 1.4.1: "The student will demonstrate the ability to identify different kinds of housing."
CASAS 1.4.2: "...interpret classified ads and other information to locate housing."
CASAS 1.4.3: "...interpret lease and rental agreements."
CASAS 1.4.4: "...determine ways to obtain housing utilities."
CASAS 1.4.5: "...know about housing laws including tenant rights and anti-discrimination laws."
CASAS 1.4.7: "...read and understand information related to home maintenance.")

Beyond the Classroom, pp. 20–34.

Conversation Book, I, pp. 42–43, 46–51; II, pp. 60–64, 73–80.

English for Adult Competency, I, pp. 83–102; II, pp. 97–112.

Everyday English, I & IIB.

Lifelines, I, pp. 61–70; II, pp. 61–70; III, pp. 51–56; IV, pp. 41–48.

LifeSchool: Consumer Economics, pp. 77–343.

NHE Lifeskills, I, pp. 58–67; II, p. 21.

Notion by Notion, pp. 38–39.

Practical Vocabulary Builder, pp. 18–19.

Read Right! pp. 16–26.

Speaking of Survival, pp. 50–64.

Using the Want Ads, pp. 34–47.

Vocabulary Builder, pp. 16–17.

Vocabulary through Pictures, pp. 1–6.

Picture 13: A Bank Line

Picture 14: A Bank Desk

(CASAS 1.8.1: "The student will demonstrate the ability to identify the procedures for obtaining and using savings and checking accounts."
CASAS 1.8.2: "...identify and use the forms associated with banking services."
CASAS 1.8.3: "...know about interest."
CASAS 1.8.4: "...compare what types of loans are available through lending institutions.")

Banking Language.

Beyond the Classroom, pp. 2–18.

Conversation Book, I, p. 128; II, pp. 52–55.

English for Adult Competency, I, pp. 139–44; II, pp. 149–57.

Everyday English, I & IIB.

Lifelines, I, pp. 21–30; II, pp. 21–30; III, pp. 21–26; IV, pp. 15–20.

LifeSchool: Consumer Economics, pp. 595–667.

Make Your Money Grow.

NHE Lifeskills, I, pp. 69–72; II, pp. 7, 12, 17, 42, 91–93.

Notion by Notion, pp. 76–77.

Practical Vocabulary Builder, p. 2.

Read Right! pp. 108–24.

Speaking of Survival, pp. 98–112.

Picture 15: At an Airport

Picture 16: Inside a Terminal

(CASAS 2.2.2: "The student will demonstrate the ability to recognize and utilize signs connected with transportation."
CASAS 2.2.3: "...identify different types of transportation and how to use them."
CASAS 2.2.4: "...interpret transportation schedules and calculate fares."
CASAS 2.2.5: "...use maps related to travel needs."
CASAS 2.6.3: "...request information on, and make, travel and overnight accommodation reservations.")

Beyond the Classroom, pp. 159–75.

Conversation Book, I, p. 113; II, pp. 40–43.

English for Adult Competency, I, pp. 78–81; II, pp. 81–82.

English That Works, II, pp. 42–83.

Lifelines, I, pp. 31–39; II, pp. 31–39.

Lifestyles, I, pp. 57–58.

NHE Lifeskills, I, p. 26.

Notion by Notion, pp. 44–45.

Practical Vocabulary Builder, p. 7.

Read Right! pp. 46–51.

Reading Schedules, pp. 57–63.

Vocabulary Builder, p. 19.

Vocabulary through Pictures, p. 18.

Picture 17: Motor Vehicle Registration

Picture 18: A Driving Test

(CASAS 1.9.1: "The student will demonstrate the ability to interpret highway and freeway signs."
CASAS 1.9.2: "...interpret driving regulations necessary to obtain a driver's license."
CASAS 1.9.3: "...compute mileage and gasoline consumption."
CASAS 1.9.5: "...identify factors affecting the selection and purchase of a car."
CASAS 1.9.6: "...identify factors associated with the maintenance of an automobile."
CASAS 1.9.7: "...identify necessary procedures in case of automobile emergencies."
CASAS 1.9.8: "...read and interpret information associated with automobile insurance."

CASAS 2.5.7: "...interpret information about permit and license requirements.")

Be Ad-Wise, pp. 60–63.

Becoming a Driver.

Beyond the Classroom, pp. 69–80.

Conversation Book, I, pp. 108–10; II, pp. 45–57.

English for Adult Competency, I, pp. 74–77; II, pp. 83–95.

Insure Yourself.

Lifelines, III, pp. 27–42; IV, pp. 21–34.

LifeSchool: Community Resources, pp. 113–65.

More Pictures That Teach Words, pp. 6, 7, 18.

NHE Lifeskills, I, pp. 80–84; II, pp. 90, 95.

Notion by Notion, pp. 46–47.

Practical Vocabulary Builder, pp. 8–10.

Read Right! pp. 52–60.

Speaking of Survival, pp. 139–41.

Picture 19: A Furniture Store

Picture 20: The Credit Office of a Furniture Store

(CASAS 1.3.2: "The student will demonstrate the ability to interpret applications for credit, their cost and consumer responsibility."
CASAS 1.3.3: "...identify and compute different methods of financing the purchase of goods and services."
CASAS 1.5.2: "...plan for major purchases."
CASAS 1.5.3: "...interpret bills."
CASAS 1.6.2: "...identify the resources available to the consumer when confronted with misleading and/or fraudulent tactics."
CASAS 1.6.3: "...identify advertising propaganda techniques such as bait-and-switch.")
CASAS 1.7.4: "...relate maintenance procedures for household appliances and personal possessions."

Be Ad-Wise.

Beyond the Classroom, pp. 36–49.

Conversation Book, I, pp. 46–51; II, pp. 62–63, 95–96.

Credit Language.

Know Your Rights.

Lifelines, IV, pp. 34–40.

LifeSchool: Consumer Economics, pp. 63–140, 347–410, 539–93.

More for Your Money.

Speaking of Survival, pp. 178–92.

Vocabulary Builder, p. 17.

Vocabulary through Pictures, pp. 4, 5.

Picture 21: School Registration

Picture 22: A Parent-Teacher Conference

CASAS 2.3.9: "...identify child care services in the community."
(CASAS 2.5.5: "The student will demonstrate the ability to identify education and vocational services found in the community including vocational testing and counseling services."
CASAS 3.5.7: "...identify child rearing practices and community resources available to assist in the development of parenting skills.")

Conversation Book, I, p. 102.

English for Adult Competency, I, pp. 165–66, 170; II, pp. 166–67.

Everyday English, I & IA.

Practical Vocabulary Builder, p. 1.

Read Right! pp. 93–107.

Speaking of Survival, pp. 194–208.

Vocabulary Builder, p. 20.

4. Using American Names

It's useful to post lists of American names (male, female, first, last, and nicknames) in your classroom. Make the lists large, on sheets of newsprint; write with something that can be seen clearly, such as a marking pen. These lists can familiarize students with a variety of American names and can serve as possibilities for use during discussion of the pictures. They can also be a ready reference for you when you devise on-the-spot drills, stories, or examples. Depending on the names you choose, use of the lists can further focus on phonological challenges for the class: Allen/Ellen, John/Joan, Nell/Ned, and so on. If you want to individualize oral work, you can have the more able students use names that are harder to pronounce while the less able students use the easier names.

In making the lists, plan to write no more than twenty or so names on each sheet. To begin, make a list for yourself, in alphabetical order, of all the names you can think of. Then select about twenty names from that list, keeping in mind your students' pronunciation difficulties. (Indochinese students, for example, may have p/f pronunciation problems. You might include Phyllis, Frank, Patty, and Paul, among other names to practice.)

Be sure that the list of last names reflects the ethnic diversity in your class and/or area. Consider what kinds of names your students will encounter in life-skills settings. In San Francisco, my Indochinese students have trouble pronouncing Garcia, and my Spanish speakers have trouble with Nguyen. Since both last names are common in our area, both are on my list—along with Johnson, Miller, Smith, and Olsen. (To many of my Chinese-speaking students, I am "Julie Ocean.")

5. Information Gap Activities

Another pathway to using LOOK AGAIN PICTURES is that of information gap activities. These type of activities work especially well with advanced classes and in workshops for teachers. To begin with, choose a picture-pair to copy. Label the top picture "A" and the bottom picture "B." Make 1 1/2 times as many copies as you have people in your class or workshop. Cut up the copies so that you have a stack of A pictures and a stack of B pictures (NOTE: Only cut up 1/2 as many copies as there are people. Leave the remaining copies uncut.) Then proceed with the following steps:

1. Put everyone into A–B pairs (or groups of four, with two people collaborating on A and two people collaborating on B). A's and B's must be facing each other, with an upright folder or book between them (this acts as a barrier so player A can't see what player B has, and vice versa).

2. Give an A picture to the A players and a B picture to the B players. Remind the players not to look at the other person's picture!

3. Set a time limit (10–15 minutes) in which the A's and B's talk to each other. They must describe their pictures and ask each other questions until they can figure out some or all of the differences (of course, this is without seeing the other's pictures!).

4. At the end of the time limit, debrief the entire group. Make sure everyone gets an uncut copy of the A-B page. Use of an overhead transparency at this point may be helpful (see *Appendix 6*, p. 110). Some people may have questions on how to describe certain aspects of the pictures.

6. Using Overhead Projectors and Transparencies

Overhead projectors are available in most schools, but until recently they went largely unused. This was because picture transparencies were so time-consuming to prepare or expensive to buy.

Today, however, you can make transparencies with most copy machines, just like you make photocopies. So literally anything that's on a flat surface—printed matter, drawings, and black-and-white photos from magazines, newspapers, or your photo collection—can be copied onto a transparency. (Color pictures often can be copied too; but since colors translate into different shades of gray, the transparencies that result are not as clear as those made from black-and-white originals.)

There are several advantages to using projected transparencies as visuals:

1. Unlike slides, they don't require a completely darkened room in order to be shown.

2. Unlike posters or other prepared visuals, they can be made any size to suit the occasion: Simply move the projector back and forth, and adjust the focus. (A rolling cart for your projector is a must. You can wheel it in and out of your way in a flash, and turn it quickly to project on any wall.)

Forget about standing screens. Use empty spaces on walls, a pulled-down map with blank side out, tacked-up newsprint sheets, backs of posters on the wall, or a pull-down screen mounted on the wall or blackboard.

Because the transparency is projected from a flat surface, you can add information to it. You can write on it to indicate or identify parts of the picture. Or you can draw on it to add new elements to the picture. Colored pens are available for this purpose; however, since many of them are indelible, it's preferable to use erasable wax pencils that are designed to be used with overhead projectors.

You can mask part of the transparency if you want to focus on one part of the picture. Even the thinnest sheet of paper will block the light; however, 5x8 cards are easier to manipulate.

You can also add to the picture by inserting cut-out figures that can be moved around like puppets, using the eraser-end of a pencil. Select any of the group scenes in this book—the lines waiting at the bank, the bus, or the motor vehicle registration office, for instance—and insert a cardboard character that is identified as one of your students. Then begin: "Okay, Manh. This is you, standing right here next to this lady. What are you going to say to her?" In fact, if you actually *photograph* your students standing with visual space between them, you can get photo prints that can then be cut apart and added to a picture before it is duplicated or made into a transparency. When you put a cut-out picture of a particular student into any scene in this book, interesting things can happen to motivate tuned-out students or those with learning disabilities.

If you have access to overhead projector and photocopy equipment, and if you give yourself some time to experiment, you will find many other possibilities for this exciting medium.

If you don't have a projector, start asking for one. Nicely. Again and again. Find out when the next order for equipment goes in, and keep slipping in requests. Some administrators say they don't order certain pieces of equipment because nobody asks for them. So keep asking! Get your colleagues to help you.

Important: Most photocopiers (Xerox, Canon, and others) will make transparencies. BUT different models take different kinds of transparency material. Thermographic copiers (Thermofax, 3M, and others) also make transparencies. To determine the correct transparency product number to use in ordering transparency material for your machines, check with the company that services your copier and supplies your office equipment. Using the wrong transparency material can jam or damage your copying equipment.

Many ideas here are the grandchildren of ideas presented several years ago by Marge Ryder and K. Lynn Savage/SFCCD, in their reports on conference presentations by Mark Seng, University of Texas.

Look Again Pictures

7. A Short List of Handy ESL References

Language

Clear Speech. By Gilbert. New York: Cambridge University Press, 1984.

English Sentence Structures. By Krohn. Ann Arbor: University of Michigan Press, 1970.

English Usage. By Marquez and Bowen. Rowley, Mass.: Newbury House, 1983.

Functions of American English: Communication Activities for the Classroom. By Jones and von Baeyer. New York: Cambridge University Press, 1983.

Gambits: Conversational Tools. Vol. I (1976), Vol. II (1976), Vol. III (1979). By Keller and Warner. Canadian Government Publishing Centre, Supply and Services Canada, Hull, Quebec. K1A OS9. Cat. nos.: (Vol. I) SC3–52/1976–1; (Vol. II) SC3–52/1976–2; (Vol. III) SC3–52/1979–3.

Manual of American English Pronunciation. By Prator and Robinett. New York: Holt, Rinehart and Winston, 1970.

Patterns of English Pronunciation. By Bowen. Rowley, Mass.: Newbury House, 1975.

Sounds Easy!, Consonants Sound Easy!, Initial Clusters Sound Easy!, Final Clusters Sound Easy! By Bassano. Hayward, Ca.: Alemany Press, 1980, 1983.

*The ESL Miscellany. A Cultural and Linguistic Inventory of American English. By Clark, Moran, and Burrows. Brattleboro, Vt.: Pro Lingua Associates, 1981.

The Grammar Book: An ESL/EFL Teacher's Course. By Celce-Murcia and Larsen-Freeman. Rowley, Mass.: Newbury House, 1983.

The PD's: Pronunciation/Aural Discrimination Drills for Learners of English. By Trager and Henderson. Englewood Cliffs, N.J.: Prentice-Hall, 1956.

The PD's in Depth. By Trager. Englewood Cliffs, N.J.: Prentice-Hall, 1982.

Understanding and Using English Grammar. By Azar. Englewood Cliffs, N.J.: Prentice-Hall, 1981.

An Overview of the Field of ESL/EFL

Principles and Practices of Language Learning and Teaching. By Brown. Englewood Cliffs, N.J.: Prentice-Hall, 1980.

The Natural Approach: Language Acquisition in the Classroom. By Krashen and Terrell. Hayward, Ca.: Alemany Press, 1983.

Techniques and Methods: Collections

Bench Marks in Reading. By Rathmell. Hayward, Ca.: Alemany Press, 1984.

Bridge the Gap: A Guide to the Development of Acquisition Activities. By Ferrer and de Poleo. Hayward, Ca.: Alemany Press, 1983.

*Classroom Practices in Adult ESL. By Ilyin and Tragardh. Washington, D.C.: TESOL (Teachers of English to Speakers of Other Languages), 1980.

*Communication-Starters and Other Activities for the ESL Classroom. By Olsen. Hayward, Ca.: Alemany Press, 1977. (Contains maps for duplication.)

Language Teaching Games and Contests. By Lee. New York: Oxford University Press, 1977.

*Language Teaching Techniques. By Clark. Brattleboro, Vt.: Pro Lingua Associates, 1980.

Look Who's Talking. By Christison and Bassano. Hayward, Ca.: Alemany Press, 1981.

Teaching English as a Second or Foreign Language. By Celce-Murcia and McIntosh. Rowley, Mass.: Newbury House, 1979.

Texts with Interesting Approaches and Techniques

Alice Blows a Fuse: Fifty Strip Stories in English. By Boyd and Boyd. Englewood Cliffs, N.J.: Prentice-Hall, 1980.

Connections: Communicative Listening and Speaking Activities. By Boyd and Boyd. New York: Regents, 1981.

Drawing Out: Second Language Acquisition through Student-Created Images. By Bassano and Christison. Hayward, Ca.: Alemany Press, 1982.

From Acceptance to Zeal. By Akiyama. New York: Minerva Books, 1981.

Getting Along in English. By Palmer and Kimball. New York: Longman, 1981.

Improving Aural Comprehension. By Morley. Ann Arbor: University of Michigan Press, 1972.

---

*Novice teachers will find it helpful to start with these books. More experienced teachers will also find them useful.

Listening Dictation: Understanding English Sentence Structure. By Morley. Ann Arbor: University of Michigan Press, 1976.

Listening for Structural Cues. By Messerschmitt. Hayward, Ca.: Alemany Press, 1981.

Listening In and Speaking Out. Intermediate (1980); Advanced (1981). By Bode *et al.* New York: Longman, 1980, 1981.

Live Action English for Foreign Students. By Romijn and Seely. Hayward, Ca.: Alemany Press, 1979.

Notional Functional Exercises with the Mini-Check System. By Messerschmitt and Zhao. Hayward, Ca.: Alemany Press, 1982.

Side by Side. Bks I & II. By Molinsky and Bliss. Englewood Cliffs, N. J.: Prentice-Hall, 1980.

Story Squares: Fluency in English as a Second Language. By Knowles and Sasaki. Boston: Little, Brown & Co., 1980.

Talking Behind Masks: Socio-Drama for ESL Students. By Grout. Hayward, Ca.: Alemany Press, 1983.

Ten Steps: A Course in Controlled Composition for Beginning and Intermediate ESL Students. By Brookes and Withrow. New York: Language Innovations, 1974.

Twenty-Six Steps: A Course in Controlled Composition for Intermediate and Advanced ESL Students. By Kunz. New York: Language Innovations, 1972.

Write Me a Ream: A Course in Controlled Composition. By Kunz and Viscount. New York: Teacher's College Press, 1973.